RECIPES
from the
FRENCH WINE
HARVEST

VINTAGE FEASTS FROM THE VINEYARDS

RECIPES
from the
FRENCH WINE
HARVEST

VINTAGE FEASTS FROM THE VINEYARDS

Rosi Hanson

Photographs by
Katerina Kalogeraki

SEVEN
DIALS

First published in the United Kingdom in 1995 by
Cassell

This paperback edition first published in 2000 by
Seven Dials, Cassell & Co
Wellington House, 125 Strand
London, WC2R 0BB

Created and produced by
Rosemary Wilkinson Publishing

Distributed in the United States of America by
Sterling Publishing Co., Inc.
387 Park Avenue South,
New York, NY 10016-8810

A CIP catalogue record for this book is available
from the British Library

ISBN 1 84188 098 1

Design: Pentrix Design
Copy editor: Jay Hornsby
Colour reproduction: Master Image Pte Ltd, Singapore
Printed in Hong Kong

CONTENTS

For Anthony and Christopher, with love

Acknowledgements

It was a conversation with Bernadette Raveneau, Anne-Françoise Lafarge and Marielle Grivot that triggered off this book. Preparing a *boeuf à la mode* for a large party of growers, customers and wine-writers following a tasting of Burgundies, we got talking about the wine-harvest and the work of feeding the pickers. The idea was like a newly-planted vine which takes at least four years to produce fruit.

I am particularly grateful to those Burgundian friends and indeed to all the wine-making families described in the text. On many occasions I met several generations who generously gave their recipes, anecdotes and culinary tips, hospitably opening bottles and inviting me to share meals.

I would especially like to thank those who allowed me to hang about their harvest kitchens, asking questions, when they were at their busiest and those who made it possible for us to photograph work in the vines, vat-houses and kitchens at such a nerve-racking time.

During several harvests I had many conversations with pickers and I am grateful to all those who took the time to share their experiences.

Many other people contributed either by giving contacts or background information. In particular, my grateful thanks go to Gerald Asher, Madame Simon Bize, Charles and Marie-France Blagdon, William and Trudy Bolter, Michel Cestia, Mme Serge Dagueneau, Cathie Faller, the Franquet-Monthelon family, Gillian Mawrey, Christian Moueix, Mme Henri Richou, Patrick and Sachiko Saulnier Blache and Peter Wasserman.

I would like to thank Sandy McArthur for her help during a research trip to the Loire and Katrina Erskine and James Anderson for their help and hospitality during a trip to the Rhône. Becky Wasserman and Russell Hone were most generous, kindly allowing us to cook recipes and photograph them in their Bouilland home, as well as giving much useful information and encouragement.

For help with recipe research and much else I particularly want to thank Bart Wasserman. Several friends were stalwart in testing and re-testing recipes - Ken Blakely, Jonathan Courage, Elizabeth Shirreff, Augusta Skidelsky and Paul Wasserman - and I thank them all. I also thank my son, Christopher Hanson for eating and making constructive comments on all the recipes.

I owe a great deal to Rosemary Wilkinson for believing in the original idea and for her help in bringing the book to completion, and to photographer Katerina Kalogeraki for her patience and skill, working in taxing conditions. I much appreciated Jay Hornsby's expert editing and Mike Spiller's valuable design contribution.

Finally, I owe the greatest debt of thanks to my husband, Anthony Hanson MW. I have been able to draw on his thirty years' experience of wine-trading and, as ever, he has been more than generous in sharing his knowledge. Without him I would never have met the growers, picked the harvests, drunk the wines or eaten the food that inspired the book; without his constant encouragement I would not have finished it.

INTRODUCTION

Everywhere the smell of wine in the making, and underfoot in little towns and villages a mess of discarded stalks and grape-skins - it is the wine-harvest. All over France, from the Rhone valley in the south to the northern vineyards of Alsace, people are busy in the vines, vat-houses and harvest kitchens.

The scenery is lovely, the mood lively. Behind the names and vintages of great wines revered around the world are real people, working in the heat or the rain, suffering from blisters and backache, and the odd hang-over, meeting up with old friends, making new ones, determined to get the most out of their two week escape from routine. They come from all walks of life, taking their annual holiday to pick the grapes. Professors work alongside train-drivers, ski instructors with bands of itinerant gypsies; students come from all over the world, earn some money and get a taste of French culture they never forget. Far-flung members of the vineyard-owning families come home to help. Holding it all together, creating the ambiance, are the cooks.

This is their story - their skill and resourcefulness and their great good humour - as well as their recipes. The day usually starts at 6 a.m., does not finish until 10 p.m. or later and when they finally fall into bed, they are likely to be kept awake by partying pickers. Their work will be frequently interrupted - perhaps a young picker has gashed a finger as he or she clips the bunches of grapes with the secateurs and needs stitches. They are regularly called upon to minister to pickers suffering from sunstroke, or gastric problems, or to sort out the language difficulties of any foreign students in the team, not to mention acting as agony-aunts to the love-sick. Often they have the responsibility of keeping account of who has worked what hours, paying them accordingly at the end of each week and dealing with the accompanying tiresome paperwork. It is they who keep up the morale among the wine-makers, cossetting the cavistes with cakes when, anxious as the mother of a newborn baby, they tear themselves away from the vat-house for late-night snacks.

Feeding the harvesters is a tour de force, but the recipes are ones we can all use. Very few of the cooks are professionals: usually they are the mothers, wives or sisters of the growers, helped by friends or vineyard employees. There are lessons to be learned here. These cooks manage to keep to a strict budget. They use ingredients which are good value - whatever is plentiful in their own kitchen gardens or local shops and markets - to make traditional old favourites. They turn left-overs into delicious meals. Most of them keep notes of menus, recipes, quantities and cost, from harvest to harvest, then hand them on to the next generation as it takes over.

At quiet times of the year I have sat at the kitchen tables of many of these ladies, delving into dog-eared notebooks which one day will be an important social record as the traditions of rural life are eroded. Filled with details of who was there and what the weather was like during the vintage, with photographs stuck in from time to time and reminders to 'use the big black casserole for this', 'use salsify if not enough mushrooms', they bring the vintage richly to life.

In some villages these harvest traditions are dying. No pickers need feeding when the vintage has been mechanized, nor do regional dishes always survive intact when young growers employ outside caterers to organize the food. But these eminently practical country recipes migrate most smoothly to town kitchens and modern lifestyles, where I hope they may take on a new life.

BURGUNDY

Burgundy is a large region composed of four departements, the Yonne, the Nièvre, the Côte d'Or and Saone et Loire but when wine lovers say 'Burgundy' they often mean the 'Côte d'Or' - the golden slope. Elsewhere in Burgundy a great deal of good wine is made, notably in Beaujolais and Mâconnais, and, increasingly good value, on the Côte Chalonnaise and around Mercurey, but it is the Côte d'Or which is most prestigious in terms of world renown.

◄ *The Côte d'Or near Puligny-Montrachet*

The Côte d'Or is divided in two halves, known as the Côte de Beaune and the Côte de Nuits. Geographically it is astonishingly small. As you drive along the N74 from Dijon to Chagny, on one side of the road is a band of perfectly oriented vineyards on limestone soil, on the other the plain, where the few vines that are planted produce an everyday-drinking wine, and you are more likely to see other crops. Passing the villages on the 'right' side of the road is like reading one of the world's most expensive wine-lists; names like Gevrey-Chambertin, Chambolle-Musigny, Vosne-Romanée, Nuits-St Georges, Aloxe-Corton, Beaune, Pommard and Meursault are just a selection.

Many of these villages have taken the name of their best *Grand Cru* vineyard - for example, the village of Gevrey added Chambertin, the name of its most famous *Grand Cru* (thus confusing consumers all over the world who may pay a lot for a bottle of Gevrey-Chambertin, thinking they are getting Le Chambertin).

The wine labels of Burgundy are notoriously complicated. The easiest way to understand the different levels of quality is to visualize a pyramid. Start at the base: the bottom half of the pyramid is made up of regional wines - on the label it will say Beaujolais, or Mâcon Blanc, or Bourgogne Rouge, for example. Going up the steps of the pyramid, in terms of quality, next come wines from an individual village, like Pommard, or Chambolle-Musigny. Within each village a band of vineyards has been classified First Growths (*Premier Crus*). On their labels they are allowed to put, first the village name, then the vineyard in letters of the same size, i.e. Pommard Les

A regional label - Bourgogne Rouge

Epenots, or Chambolle-Musigny Les Amoureuses. You might think that First Growths were the best wines, that is after all the case in Bordeaux, but not in Burgundy. The greatest vineyards of Burgundy, and now we reach the peak of our pyramid, where the volume produced is tiny, are the Great Growths (*Grands Crus*), i.e. Le Musigny, or Le Corton, Le Chambertin, Le Montrachet, and so on.

All this is further complicated by the fact that, unlike most wine-growing areas, Burgundy's vineyards are split up among many owners. The Great Growth, Clos Vougeot, is a famous example, with its eighty or so owners, each cultivating their rows of vines and vinifying their wine in their own way. Owners of some of the finest estates (domaines) may have rows of vines in a number of the Great Growth or First Growth vineyards of several neighbouring villages.

It is rare for a family to live in a large house or château surrounded by their vines as is the case in Bordeaux. Estates are small: a typical estate supporting a family might be just ten to fifteen acres. Land changes hands rarely and then for astronomical prices. Wine-making remains essentially a family business, with sons and daughters taking over from their parents in gradual succession.

There are two grape varieties producing the finest wines: Pinot Noir for the reds and Chardonnay for the whites. The white Aligoté grape produces a lighter, fresher wine mainly drunk locally and the Gamay is planted throughout the Beaujolais, giving a youthful, fruity, red wine. In Chablis, in northern Burgundy, is another pocket of expensive and sought-after white wines.

*Examples of Grand Cru (top)
and Premier Cru labels*

Pinot noir grapes ready to be loaded onto the tractor

The grape is again the Chardonnay.

The beautiful town of Beaune is the undisputed capital of Burgundy's wine marketing, and one of the most visited of all France's historic sites. Layers of history, from prehistoric to Roman to Renaissance, make this a fascinating architectural study, quite apart from the town's long connection with wine. (There is a museum of wine, the *Musée du Vin*.) The old walls are partly intact and at the centre is the jewel in historic Beaune's crown, the Hospices de Beaune, founded in 1443 by Nicholas Rolin for the benefit of the poor and the sick, with its spectacular and much photographed, coloured, tiled roof. On the way to the flourishing Saturday market, glimpses of these tiles are a special pleasure.

Equally spectacular is the auction which is held each year of the Hospices' wines. Over the centuries the charity has been endowed with an impressive estate of vineyards, the wines from which are sold each November. This event is the centrepiece of 'Les Trois Glorieuses', which draws crowds, including buyers from all over the world, to enjoy a jamboree of banquets, tastings and wine-gossip.

FEEDING THE PICKERS

Picking machines are hardly ever seen in the Côte d'Or and pickers often come from far afield, returning year after year to the same estates. Food plays a large part in this fidelity, with pickers requesting their favourite dishes every year, dishes like *pot-au-feu* (see page 32) or *crapaudine*, a Burgundian dish in which layers of sliced potatoes, pork fat and grated Gruyère cheese are baked slowly in a large cast-iron casserole (see page 38). Perhaps they like these old-fashioned recipes not only because they are sustaining but also because they are the real *cuisine familiale*, or home cooking, which few people are lucky enough to eat these days.

Around the end of May, beginning of June, wine-makers are afflicted with the kind of restless anxiety usually found in women awaiting the birth of a child. They are waiting for the flowering of the vines. It is crucial. Will it pass smoothly? Or will a year's work be ruined by strong winds, violent rain or even hail? If all goes well and they can walk among their vines inhaling the faint, sweet smell of the little white flowers, they can heave a sigh of relief and start calculating, roughly at least, the dates of the harvest. At this moment many growers' wives are already thinking about how they will feed the harvesters.

The harvest cook has to think ahead to the time when she transforms herself into a restaurant manager and chef

Pickers in the Lafarge's vines in Volnay

Homemade preserves - beans, fruit, and jams - in the Raveneaus' cellar

Mme Raveneau (right) and helper, preparing salad for the pickers' lunch

calls for a *dessert elabouré* - a *gâteau roulé* perhaps (see page 45), for which that homemade jam is useful, or a *gâteau aux pommes* (see page 45).

The final preparations take about ten days. Many wine-makers have a house, shut up most of the year, where pickers are lodged. Usually simple, shabby almost, with lino on the floor and only the bare essentials, it will be scrubbed and cleaned until it is spotless.

The cook will have consulted her notebook with its lists of menus and quantities from previous years and prepared her shopping lists, working always two or three days in advance for basic supplies.

Once the harvest begins, the cook's day starts at about 5.30 a.m. when she prepares breakfast. At 6.15 she may go up the road to the baker for the fresh *baguettes*. At 6.30 she wakes the pickers - the whole thing is timed like a military operation. Breakfast, usually consisting of a choice of tea, coffee or hot chocolate, cereals with milk, perhaps collected from a nearby farm, then fresh bread and butter and jams, is served from 6.45 until the trucks arrive at 7.15 to take the picking team to the vines.

By the the time she has cleared the refectory - a rather grand name for the simple rooms with concrete floors and trestle tables that are the norm - the cook is more than glad to sit down in peace to her own breakfast and spend half an hour thinking and planning the day.

In the vines work starts promptly. The foreman deploys his workers, handing out secateurs and paniers and allotting rows to those who will cut the grapes. Bigger containers are given to the *hotteurs* whose job it is to hop over the lines of vines collecting the grapes from the pickers, and empty them onto the trucks waiting to take them to the vat-house.

rolled into one. The trick is *l'intendance*, being organized, having a plan of campaign. Many grow their own vegetables and fruit so, earlier in the year, the cook makes sure enough potatoes are sown and that there will be enough herbs and salad in the garden for when they are needed. She grows plenty of tomatoes, peeling and bottling some, preparing and freezing others ready for pizzas. The biggest of the crop will end up on the harvest menu as *tomates farcies* (see page 37), so they are frozen, as soon as they ripen, the insides having been scooped out to be used in soups and sauces. As they come into season she bottles or freezes *haricots verts* and makes jam from soft fruit to use for the harvesters' breakfast. Many harvest cooks make and preserve terrines and pâtés which come in handy for evening meals. These usually start with soup, followed by cold meats, a hot vegetable dish, green salad, cheese and a simple dessert like a fruit compote, unless a picker's birthday or a saint's day is being celebrated: this

In the early morning mist voices are muffled; the pickers soon have arms soaked in dew, as they part the leaves looking for the bunches of grapes; later blisters will start,

A First Growth Chablis label

aggravated by the sweet grape juice which makes hands sticky, and backs start to ache from bending over the vines. Gathering the harvest is hard work and food-breaks keep the pickers going. The first, a second breakfast in the vines, is particularly welcome to warm everyone up.

In the kitchen the cook and her helpers start early on the lunch, which often features traditional dishes needing long, slow simmering. Although sometimes eaten outside in the vines, lunch is a substantial meal and certainly not

a picnic. The main dish is usually preceded by a salad and followed by cheese, fruit or yogurt. Preparations for the lunch are interrupted while they pack the second breakfast or *casse croûte* into a van to go to the vineyard at about 8.30 or 9.00.

After lunch at mid-day the picking starts again at 1.30 and continues until 5.30, when the exhausted team is brought back, eager for a cold drink, a snack, a wash and a rest. There is only a short rest, however, for the kitchen

Bernadette Raveneau deglazing a pan on her wood-fired stove

The Raveneaus serving boeuf braisé and crapaudine to their pickers

team between clearing up lunch and preparing dinner. Restored by the evening meal, the pickers are usually in party mood but, as soon as dinner is cleared and the kitchen left clean for the next day, the cooks are ready to fall into bed.

This onerous schedule is still embraced by many Burgundians, but traditions are dying. Each year fewer estates lodge their pickers, preferring to use local people who go home in the evening. Wives of the younger generation of growers are not always able to take on the cooking if they have full-time careers of their own. Someone who is well-placed to watch this evolving pattern is Marie-Thérèse Meurgey, wife of a wine-broker and for twenty years Adjoint-Maire (Deputy Mayor) of Beaune. Her face lights up when we talk about harvest meals and she begins to reminisce about her own childhood in the Mâconnais, recommending *fromage fort* (literally, 'strong cheese', a kind of cheese paste - see page 29) - 'this was something often made for the harvest - it is wonderful!'

What follows are the stories and recipes of some of those wine-makers who, still, as Marie-Thérèse says, really make the harvest into a celebration.

CASSE-CROUTE IN
THE CHABLIS VINEYARDS

Domaine Jean-Marie Raveneau's wines are found on the wine lists of the world's most renowned restaurants. To meet a worldwide demand there is only a small amount of wine bearing the great names of the best Chablis vineyards so they are expensive, but wine writers and wine-lovers agree that Jean-Marie's white wines are the *crème de la crème*.

At 8.30 in the morning the slopes of Chablis are still enveloped in mist and the pickers are wet and cold. A bundle of dry vine-shoots, the product of earlier pruning, is waiting to make a small bonfire to warm them up during the break for the *casse-croûte*.

The Raveneau's Deux-Chevaux van bumps its way up the chalky, unsurfaced road to the *Grand Cru* vineyard called Blanchot, high above the little town which, normally sleepy, has been thrown into action by the harvest. The workers finish their rows as the plastic bottle-carrier of *vin rouge* and the basket filled with the picnic of crusty *baguettes* (French long loaves), marinated herrings, salami sausage, Camembert cheese and a big slab of dark chocolate are lifted out of the van and the fire is lit.

The pickers stand around the fire at the edge of the vineyard, stamping their feet, eating and knocking back tumblers of the rough wine. Someone produces an ancient Opinel penknife to hack off the slices of salami. The vinegary raw herring goes down surprisingly well after the early morning start. As they warm up, some of them cross the little road to a grassy bank where they can sit and smoke in the weak sunlight which is beginning to penetrate the mist.

The fire dies down and Jean-Marie Raveneau puts a small grill over the embers. He breaks off a piece of *baguette*, splits it open and toasts it a little on the grill. Then he makes a sandwich of it with a piece of dark chocolate and puts it back on the fire until the chocolate begins to melt into the bread. 'It's delicious, but you must have it with this.' One of Jean-Marie's cellar-workers has

just arrived with the tractor and trailer from the vat-house. He passes round a venerable-looking bottle, ratafia, a wine fortified with *marc* or brandy, to go with the *pain au chocolat*.

The Raveneaus' vendange house: the entrance to the cellars, on the right, is a hazard to carousing pickers

MADAME LAFARGE'S POT-AU-FEU

On the Côte de Beaune, in Volnay, which is renowned for its red wines, Michel Lafarge is supervising the arrival of the grapes in the *cuverie* or vat-house. This family makes a range of mainly red wines from Bourgogne Rouge to village Volnay to First Growths like Beaune Grèves and Volnay Clos des Chênes. The streets of the small village are blocked by *tracteurs enjambeurs* (the special long-legged tractors made to straddle the rows of vines) pulling their loads of grape-filled crates from the vineyards. Now, at mid-day, it is rush-hour as the trucks bring the pickers down from the surrounding slopes.

Madame Lafarge finishes supervising the laying of the table as the harvesters are hosing down their muddy boots. Salads are on the table for the first course; in the kitchen the windows are steamed up as the *pot-au-feu* simmers. A fresh tomato sauce is being prepared to go with it; the cook is putting the cooked tomatoes and plenty of parsley through a large food-mill.

By the time the *pot-au-feu* has been cleared and the cheese is on the table, the pickers are relaxed and start singing. 'This group is always singing,' says Noëlle Lafarge, smiling. 'Most of them come from the same village in the Bresse and they all know each other - in fact most of them are related - so the atmosphere is good. One man has been coming for twenty years - we're

Lafarge grapes arriving at the Volnay vat-house

having a little celebration tonight, but don't say anything because it's a surprise. It's strange after the *vendanges* - suddenly it's just Michel and me for supper - it hardly seems worth cooking such small quantities!'

Many of the people I spoke to are experts in *l'art d'accomoder les restes*, that wonderfully French way of economically turning left-overs into something special. Chez Lafarge they use up the left-overs from the *pot-au-feu* in a *pain de viande* the following day at supper. It is served as a first course with a tomato sauce, and followed by a herb omelette, green salad, cheese and a dessert of home-bottled cherries in syrup. The *pain de viande* is made by mincing the cold beef and mixing it with enough egg and cream to make it moist. Chopped onion and parsley are added before putting the mixture into a soufflé dish and baking it in a moderate oven for about 30 minutes. It is unmoulded and served hot with the tomato sauce in a

separate sauce-boat or bowl. This economical dish is easy to make and very good.

Other favourite ways of transforming left-over meat are to mince it and use it as a filling for a *tourte* (top and bottom pie made with short pastry, see page 35), for stuffing tomatoes, or for *hachis Parmentier*, the French equivalent of cottage pie (see page 88). It is a source of pride that everything is put to good use and this can include vegetables as well as meat.

In 1992 one woman told me that she had managed to make a good supper for her pickers for only two francs a head - quite an achievement! The meal had started with *crème Dubarry*, a soup she had made from the left-overs of a cauliflower cheese added to a rather liquid Béchamel sauce, followed by stuffed tomatoes, then a *tarte aux pommes* using apples from the garden. Needless to say, she had not costed in her time.

Lunch for the pickers at the Lafarge's harvest house

LA CUISINE FAMILIALE

No Burgundian harvest is complete without the traditional *boeuf bourguignon*, says Colette Imbert, who cooks for the pickers of the Domaine Leflaive and those of the merchant Olivier Leflaive in Puligny Montrachet. The Domaine, which has vines in the *Grands Crus* of Montrachet, Chevalier-Montrachet, Bâtard-Montrachet and Bienvenues-Bâtard-Montrachet as well as other Puligny vineyards, has been in the Leflaive family for over 250 years.

Sixty or seventy people sit down to lunch together here during the harvest and Mme Imbert has a clear under-standing of what is needed. 'The harvest meals are simple but nourishing without being too heavy because the position for cutting the grapes is not particularly favourable for good digestion,' she says. 'La cuisine est donc familiale' (therefore, family dishes are what we serve).

Her lunch menu might be a green salad with hard-boiled eggs, followed by the famous *boeuf bourguignon* (see page 42) served with garlic croûtons and steamed pota-toes or a green salad with chicken livers followed by

Transferring grapes from one of the long-legged tractors to a bigger truck

escalopes de dinde à la crème (escalopes of turkey breast in cream with mushrooms, see page 40) and the meal would end with cheese and fruit. In the evening, as she says, people can take their time and the meal is more relaxed. A vegetable soup may be followed by a lentil salad and *croissants au jambon* (a slice of ham rolled up in puff pastry with plenty of grated Gruyère and baked for a few minutes in a hot oven) or by slices of raw country ham and *gratin de macaroni* (macaroni cheese, see page 61) and end with cheese and apple tart.

A little further north, on the Côte de Nuits, at the most famous of all these great Burgundian estates, the Domaine de la Romanée-Conti, meals follow a similar pattern. That Managing Director, Aubert de Villaine, is not overweight is something of a miracle for not only is the food excellent here, but equally delicious are the harvest meals at the Bouzeron domaine owned and run by him and his Californian wife. When these two estates' harvests overlap, as they must often do, Aubert must find himself hard put to choose between *coq au vin* in Vosne-Romanée or *ragoût de porc à la Bouzeronnaise* at home. (He would claim, no doubt, that he is far too busy worrying about the wine-making to think about food.)

'It's hard work, but I love the harvest,' says Pamela de Villaine whose menus include versions of traditional French recipes from the American writers Julia Child and Richard Olney as well as dishes such as stuffed potatoes, *lapin du Vertempière* (see page 41) and desserts evolved by Yves Bernard, a chef who for three years took his annual holiday to coincide with the harvest and cooked for the de Villaine's pickers.

These pickers are some of the most pampered in Burgundy - not only are they *logis et nourris* (lodged and fed) but also *blanchis*: their laundry is done for them. Dinner is often followed by multi-lingual games as their picking team includes a mixture of nationalities and there is usually someone with a guitar to encourage singing.

CELEBRATIONS

Throughout France the last load of grapes of the harvest is celebrated by decorating the tractors with flowers and branches from the vineyards and verges - sometimes gardens are raided to make a good show - and driving in convoy, with horns hooting, lights blazing, back to the vat-house. At the Lafarges' the tradition is that the last grapes are emptied into the *fouloir-égrappoir* (the machine that de-stalks and crushes the grapes) by the women pickers.

Villages often have their very local customs. In Volnay a church service is held before the harvest begins and growers bring some of their grapes to be blessed.

A tractor decorated with a motley selection of flowers and greenery to celebrate the end of the harvest

Above the village among pine trees and commanding a splendid view over the hillside of vines, the roofs of the village and across the plain, is a large statue, the Madonna of the vines. Standing here, Chantal Lafarge points out the vineyard where her husband Frédéric, son of Michel and Noëlle, is supervising the picking. After the harvest the Lafarge family will join other growers from the village, and their families, in climbing the steep path to the Madonna, a little pilgrimage after a Thanksgiving Mass in the church.

Rare is the French wine-grower who does not celebrate the end of the work and thank the team of pickers with a party. This event is known here in Burgundy as *la Paulée*. The families often invite friends and relations to join them and this copious meal usually includes the best of their repertoire of harvest dishes.

The village of Meursault has turned *la Paulée* into a rather special communal event. In the 1920s, when Burgundy wines were not selling well, a leading grower, Comte Lafon, suggested that all the growers from the village should get together, with their families and guests, among whom would be potential buyers, for a celebratory lunch. Each family would bring its best bottles to this banquet. So successful has this event become that now buyers and wine connoisseurs from all over the world vie for an invitation. *La Paulée de Meursault* forms part of the 'Trois Glorieuses' in November when the Hospices de Beaune holds the celebrated auction of its wines. The participants in Meursault's lunch rarely rise from the table, except to go into a cellar to do some tasting, before dusk and sometimes a good deal later.

From top to bottom: Salade de choux aux pommes, salade de foies blondes and carottes râpées - first courses for harvest lunches

CAROTTES RAPEES, SAUCE MOUTARDE
GRATED CARROT SALAD WITH MUSTARD VINAIGRETTE

More often than not harvest lunches start with salads such as the ones that follow. For all of these you will find that if you double the quantities, the recipe will serve about 10 people.

FOR 4 PEOPLE
3 or 4 medium carrots
1 tablespoon chopped fresh parsley

FOR THE VINAIGRETTE:
1 tablespoon Dijon mustard
4 tablespoons of groundnut or sunflower oil
1 teaspoon red or white wine vinegar
salt and black pepper

Wash, peel and grate the carrots coarsely. Wash, dry and chop the parsley.

The vinaigrette is made rather like a mayonnaise (in fact it is sometimes called a false mayonnaise). Put the tablespoon of mustard in a small bowl. Slowly, drop by drop at first, add the oil, stirring all the time to incorporate it. It can easily separate, so be cautious. (Despite this it will only take about five minutes to make.) Add the vinegar, a pinch of salt and black pepper.

Optional: a teaspoon of boiling water can be added at the end to stabilize the sauce.

Just before serving mix carrots, parsley and sauce together.

SALADE DE FOIES BLONDES
GREEN SALAD WITH WARM CHICKEN LIVERS, CROUTONS, CHEESE AND TOMATOES

Salades composées, with many possible variations, are popular first courses. This is served by Mme Imbert in Puligny Montrachet.

FOR 6 PEOPLE
250 g (8 oz) fresh or frozen chicken livers
1 batavia, escarole or frisée salad
250 g (8 oz) tomatoes
125 g (4 oz) Gruyère
1 large slice of white bread
olive or other vegetable oil
red or white wine vinegar
salt and black pepper

If you are using frozen livers, remember to thaw them completely ahead of time.

Wash and dry the salad. Cut the tomatoes in half, scoop out the seeds and discard, cut the flesh in dice. Dice the Gruyère. Put the green leaves, tomatoes and cheese in a bowl big enough to allow you to turn them in the vinaigrette.

Dice the bread and fry in a little oil until browned. Keep warm. Carefully clean the livers, cutting out any green spots and removing any filaments. If they are large, cut them in two or three pieces.

When you are ready to serve the salad, toss the livers in a little oil - about five minutes over a brisk heat should be enough, allowing them to brown on all sides but remain a little pink inside. Add the croûtons and livers to the salad.

Deglaze the hot pan with about a tablespoon of vinegar. Off the heat swirl it round, dislodging any little crunchy bits and the juices from the livers with a wooden spoon. Pour over the salad. Add about three tablespoons of oil to the pan and do the same again. Sprinkle the salad with a little salt, grind some black pepper over it, turn vigorously and serve.

SALADE DE CHOUX AUX POMMES

CABBAGE AND APPLE SALAD

When the vintage weather is hot, this salad, crunchy and slightly creamy, is refreshing.

FOR 4 PEOPLE
**1 small Dutch or Savoy cabbage
(these are the pale green, tightly packed,
hard cabbages, although the Savoy has beautiful
dark green outer leaves)
the same weight in dessert apples, such as Cox's
2 tablespoons lemon juice
3 tablespoons olive or sunflower oil
1 tablespoon fresh chopped parsley
1 tablespoon fresh chopped chives
salt and black pepper
2 tablespoons crème fraîche**

Wash the cabbage. Trim off the outer leaves, stalk and the thickest ribs. Cut into four. Soak for 10 minutes in salted water. Drain and rinse thoroughly, drain again. Slice into fine strips.

Peel the apples or leave the skin on, as preferred, then quarter and core them. Slice thinly.

Mix the lemon juice, oil, salt, black pepper and herbs together. Have the cabbage and apple ready in a bowl and mix thoroughly with this sauce.

At the last minute add the *crème fraîche* and turn the salad again. Serve straightaway.

SALADE D'ENDIVES, SAUCE MOUTARDE

CHICORY SALAD WITH MUSTARD VINAIGRETTE

It is a confusing fact that what the French call 'endive' we call chicory, and what they call 'chicorée' or 'chicorée frisée' is curly endive to us.

FOR 4 PEOPLE
**500g (1 lb), or slightly more, chicory
ingredients as for the vinaigrette on page 27**

Remove any old, wilting, outer leaves from the chicory.
Cut off the base. Cut out the inner bitter heart, which means scooping out about 3 cm (1½ in) from the base upwards with a pointed knife. Rinse and dry. Slice them in rounds of about 3 - 4 cm (1½ in). Now they are ready to mix with the mustard vinaigrette (see carrot salad instructions on page 27).

Chagny market

CELERI-RAVE REMOULADE
CELERIAC WITH MUSTARD AND LEMON VINAIGRETTE

This salad is widely available in French charcuteries but is easily made at home and makes an appetizing first course.

FOR 4 PEOPLE
1 small celeriac
1 tablespoon fresh parsley
juice of half a lemon
ingredients as before for the vinaigrette (see page 27), replacing the vinegar with lemon juice

Scrub, peel and grate the celeriac. Some people prefer to cut it into matchsticks. Mix it with a little lemon juice while you make the sauce, or it will go grey. Wash, dry and chop the parsley.

Make the sauce as in the grated carrot salad recipe on page 27. Mix all together and serve.

VARIATIONS ON CLASSIC DISHES
❖ *The celeriac may be blanched in boiling, salted water for a few minutes, drained, dried, then mixed with the sauce. Less crunchy and thought to be more digestible.*

LE FROMAGE FORT
(LITERALLY STRONG CHEESE) AS DESCRIBED BY MARIE-THERESE MEURGEY

'You take some hard goat's milk cheese, or a mixture of goat's and cow's milk cheese, and grate it. I usually put in some Gruyère, finely grated. Pour over a large glass of white wine and a little marc de Bourgogne (or brandy), add some finely chopped garlic and some soft white cheese. Use a fork to mix everything together. Leave in a bowl for 24 hours - put it somewhere cool (not as cold as a fridge as it's going to ferment a little - but not too hot either!). And that's all. You know, this is a wonderfully economic little dish - it's a good way to use up the ends of cheeses, even Camembert.

When you want to serve it, you toast some big slices of farmhouse bread and spread the fromage fort on them to finish a meal, or for the casse-croûte in the vines.'

Approximate quantities: 4 hard cow's milk cheeses to 4 hard goat's milk cheeses (you could use the small cheeses about 5 cm (2 in) in diameter that you see often in France, usually locally made and unnamed or choose a hard cheese such as Cantal mixed with some Tomme de chèvre), to 2 fresh white soft cheeses, to 1 handful of grated Gruyère.

Marie-Thérèse emphasizes that there is no correct version: the recipe accommodates whatever cheese is available and your taste, but the end result should be moist, not liquid - a spreadable paste.

This is rather like the old-fashioned English potted cheese, which was a popular way of using up the end of a Stilton or a truckle of Cheddar.

Oeuf en meurette: poached egg in a red wine sauce with garlic toast

OEUFS EN MEURETTE, OEUFS AU VIN

POACHED EGGS IN A RED WINE SAUCE

Eggs, bacon and toast - the ingredients of an English breakfast, but this could not be more Burgundian. The combination of lardons, onions and red wine is a traditional one here, featuring most famously in boeuf bourguignon and coq au vin.

The mind boggles at the idea of poaching enough eggs for the pickers of any of the larger estates but there certainly are growers who consider this to be a real harvest dish.

In the old-fashioned peasant version the use of onion and of flour is somewhat heavy-handed, and the red wine sauce is left to simmer for about three hours, presumably while the family were out in the vines. When they came home tired and hungry they only needed to poach the eggs before putting their feet up in front of the fire on which they could toast the slices of country bread rubbed with garlic. Methods have evolved to suit modern life-styles.

A note about the wine - naturally this does not call for the most expensive Grand Cru, but do not use anything you would not be happy to drink. A good Bourgogne Pinot Noir would be my choice. It may seem extravagant, but the other ingredients are cheap, and the effect is worth it. Serve the eggs either as a first course followed by something light or as a main course with a salad afterwards.

FOR 6 PEOPLE

6 fresh eggs
1 small onion
1 clove of garlic
bouquet garni (fresh parsley sprigs, thyme, fresh or dried on the branch, bay leaf, all tied together with a piece of fine string)
½ - ¾ bottle of red Burgundy
125 g (4 oz) green streaky bacon in a piece
1 tablespoon fresh, finely chopped parsley

FOR THE BEURRE MANIE:

1 teaspoon plain flour (for those who avoid wheat flour, potato flour (fécule) works well)
1 teaspoon butter at room temperature

FOR THE CROUTONS:

1 stick of French bread
1 clove garlic

Take the eggs out of the fridge so that they will be at room temperature when you need them. They should be fresh and not too large, or they will be more difficult to poach.

Peel and roughly chop the onion and one clove of garlic. Wash, dry and tie the herbs in a bunch. Put them with the wine in an enamelled saucepan and simmer uncovered for 20 minutes. Make the sure the pan is wide enough to make it easy to poach more than one egg at a time in it.

Meanwhile, prepare the *beurre manié* by mixing the flour and butter to a paste with a wooden spoon in a bowl. Leave aside, not in the fridge but not on top of the stove.

Cut the bread, one slice per person. Peel and cut the second clove of garlic in half .

Remove the rind from the bacon and cut it into dice to make the lardons. Cook over a high heat until the fat begins to run and they brown, then drain on kitchen paper and put aside until the wine has simmered for 20 minutes. Now add them to the wine, onion, garlic and herbs and simmer for a further 10 minutes. Pour the wine through a sieve into a bowl and return to the pan. From the debris in the sieve, extract the lardons and keep them warm - this is a little fiddly - maybe someone else could be delegated to do this while you poach the eggs. The same useful person could now grill the croûtons, (or they could be baked for about five minutes in a hot oven if that is more convenient), then rub both sides with the cut surface of the garlic.

Break the eggs into a teacup, one by one. Have the wine simmering briskly, but not boiling hard. Swirl the wine round with a wooden spoon. Tip in an egg, then another - two at a time is realistic for most of us. With any luck, the whites swirl round the yolks and about five minutes later you can lift them out with a skimmer, perfectly cooked, onto warmed plates. Timing will vary a bit.

When you have poached the six eggs, take the wine off the heat and quickly whisk in the *beurre manié* until smooth and shiny. Simmer for about 5 minutes, then pour over the eggs, give everyone some lardons, a garlic croûton and a little chopped parsley.

MME LAFARGE'S POT-AU-FEU

As Elizabeth David says in her book 'French Provincial Cooking' (see page 156), there is no mystery about making a pot-au-feu. It is one of those French dishes that have arisen out of the necessity to make the best use of cheap local ingredients and which have then turned into a festive and congenial way to feed a large gathering. These dishes often become imbued with folklore - then people begin to think you can only make them if certain secrets have been handed down through the generations.

Maybe the only mystery is that there is no correct version as far as ingredients go. This is basically boiled meat and vegetables. There is, perhaps, a correct method, or at least, some specific points to be made.

The first is that as the water, with the meat in it, comes to the boil, and it must do this slowly, the grey scum thrown off by the meat must be removed. This means that you must stand over the pot for about 20 minutes with a fine-mesh skimmer, removing scum as it accumulates, until what rises is whitish in colour. This is the only laborious part of the recipe.

The second point is that when the recipe says 'simmer gently' it really does mean very gently - a bubble rising to the surface every few minutes is as fast as it should go - otherwise the meat will cook too quickly and will toughen, and the broth will become cloudy. A piece of meat smaller than about 1.5 kg (3 lb) is really too small to cook in this way. The meat will shrink as it cooks.

Steaming pans of beef and vegetables - pot-au-feu for the Lafarge pickers in the making

FOR 6 - 8 PEOPLE

1 marrow bone (if possible)
1.5 kg (3 lb) piece of beef (use one of the cheaper
braising cuts, such as rolled blade or brisket,
although the latter is rather fatty)
6 black peppercorns
2 or 3 turnips, peeled and diced
6 carrots, peeled and diced
6 leeks, sliced
1 stick of celery, sliced, optional
1 onion stuck with 2 cloves
2 garlic cloves
1 bay leaf
6 sprigs parsley
2 sprigs thyme
salt

If you are able to get a marrow bone, have it cut up into manageable lengths, then tie them up in cheesecloth to prevent the marrow escaping. When the time comes to serve the dish, the marrow can be scraped out and spread on bread or toast; it is rich and delicious. If no marrow bones are available, add some beef bones for flavour, removing them at the end. Put the beef joint and the bone into a flameproof casserole with cold water (just enough to cover, not too much or you will end up with a watery broth).

Start the cooking gently, gradually bringing the water to the boil. Skim carefully until the scum turns white.

Cover the pot and let it simmer gently for at least 3 hours without interruption, except for about an hour before the end of the cooking, when you should add a few peppercorns, the prepared vegetables, the garlic, the herbs tied up in cheesecloth and salt to taste.

Serve the meat surrounded by the vegetables, with some of the broth in a separate bowl. A *pot-au-feu* is usually served with some coarse sea salt, mustard and pickled gherkins, or a fresh tomato sauce (see page 38) or an aïoli sauce (a thick garlicky mayonnaise, see page 59).

A basket of vegetables and herbs from a kitchen garden

VARIATIONS ON CLASSIC DISHES

❖ *Another method is to plunge the meat into water that is already boiling hard, to seal the meat. The method given is better if you want the meat to give more flavour to the stock .*

❖ *If you want to include cabbage, most people advise that it is best cooked separately in some of the broth which you remove from the pot. This is to avoid giving a cabbagy flavour to the rest of the broth which you may want to serve later as a soup.*

❖ *Some families serve the broth with some of the vegetables in it as a soup course, keeping the meat warm and serving it with the rest of the vegetables and some potatoes afterwards. Others serve all the vegetables and meat together, with a little of the broth to moisten them, reserving most of the broth, to which they may add some pasta or rice, for another meal.*

❖ *If you are making a pot-au-feu for a relatively small number of people (6 to 8), using a small piece of meat, you may want to increase the number of vegetables, or cook it in a beef stock instead of water. Obviously, making the dish in large quantities intensifies the flavour of the broth.*

❖ *There are so many excellent ways of using up the meat left over (e.g. pain de viande, page 23; hachis Parmentier, page 88; tourte, page 35, and as stuffings for tomatoes and other vegetables) that it is worth making more than you need for one meal. It is a very economical dish!*

❖ *In some areas, other meats, such as a piece of mutton, or a boiling fowl, or a good boiling sausage, are cooked with the meat. Everyone is then served with a selection of the meats, accompanied, as described, by the sea salt, pickles and/or sauce, depending on the local tradition.*

LE TREUFFE

A BURGUNDIAN POTATO DISH

Le Treuffé is the Burgundian patois for this potato dish. It is usually eaten with a salad as a supper dish or with meat as part of a more elaborate meal.

Use round 'soup potatoes' as the French describe them, not the long waxy ones, which they use for salads.

FOR 6 PEOPLE
500 g (1 lb) potatoes
3 eggs
2 heaped teaspoons plain flour
500 g (1 lb) white cheese, such as Ricotta, or curd cheese
2 tablespoons thick cream or crème fraîche
1 - 2 tablespoons oil, such as groundnut

Wash the potatoes but do not peel them. Cut them up if they are large but it is really better to use smaller ones and cook them whole, so that they do not become watery. Cook in boiling, salted water in their skins. When cooked, drain, and when cool enough to handle, skin them. Take a fork and mash roughly, leaving some chunks - this is not a purée.

Break the eggs into the bowl of potatoes. Sprinkle in the flour, season with salt and pepper. Mix all together. In a separate bowl, break up the white cheese, mashing it with a fork. Add this to the potato mixture with the cream. Mix together without mashing the potatoes too much. It should not be too thick a mixture but neither must it be so liquid that it pours - somewhere between the two. The potato and cheese mixture can be made ahead of time ready for the final stage just before the meal.

Heat the oil in a big frying pan. Tip in the mixture and spread it so it is like a rather thick pancake. Cook for 5 to 10 minutes over a fairly hight heat until it is brown and crisp on the bottom. Turn down the heat and continue cooking for about another 15 minutes until the mixture is firm enough to turn over and brown on the other side. The best way to do this seems to be to slide it onto a large plate, invert the pan over the plate and turn them both over. This is quite tricky as the pan is hot but the more often you do it, the easier it becomes.

Cook for another 5 to 10 minutes until the bottom of the potato cake is crisp, then slide onto a warmed plate and serve.

Vegetables and fruit against a background of bottles in the Raveneaus' root cellar

TOURTE DE VIANDE
MEAT PIE

The three recipes that follow are all useful for left-over beef from a pot-au-feu. Harvest cooks often mix it with cold roast beef and/or pork, for example. If they lack meat they top it up with sausagemeat which French butchers make with pure pork, fat and lean, ready minced. Families have their own favourite ways to do them; the following are just a guide.

A green salad would go well with this dish.

FOR 4 PEOPLE
FOR THE SHORTCRUST PASTRY:
250 g (8 oz) plain flour
1 pinch of salt
125 g (4 oz) butter at room temperature
small glass of cold water
1 egg yolk to glaze

FOR THE FILLING:
125 g (4 oz) green streaky bacon in a piece
30 g (1 oz) butter
1 medium to large onion
125 g (4 oz) sausagemeat
250 g (8 oz) boiled beef (or other left-overs)
a handful of fresh parsley
salt and black pepper

FOR THE BECHAMEL SAUCE:
30 g (1 oz) butter
30 g (1 oz) plain flour
salt and pepper
250 ml (8 fl oz) milk
nutmeg, optional

To make the pastry, mix the flour and salt in a bowl. Rub the butter into the flour with your fingertips, until it resembles breadcrumbs. Add a little cold water to make a supple dough. Form into a ball and leave in the bowl with a cloth over it to rest for an hour.

To make the filling, remove the rind from the piece of bacon. Cut the bacon in dice to make lardons. Put the butter into a large frying pan and let the bacon cook gently, melting the fat. With a slotted spoon remove the lardons and keep on one side. Peel and chop the onion. Fry it in the bacon fat and butter until it is golden, then add the sausagemeat. Mince, or if you prefer chop, the left-over meat and the lardons. Finely chop the parsley. Add these three ingredients to the frying pan. Mix together and stir as the mixture browns. Season with salt and pepper.

For the thick Béchamel, melt the butter in a saucepan. Add the flour, stirring to incorporate it. Gradually add the milk, stirring and letting the mixture thicken as you go. Season with salt and pepper. (Some might like a little grated nutmeg.) Take the mixture of meats off the heat and mix with the Béchamel.

Preheat the oven to gas mark 4, 350°F, 180°C.

Roll out the pastry, keeping back a third of it for the lid. Butter a 20 cm (8 in) pie plate or tart tin. Line it with the pastry, pressing it into the sides and letting it overlap the edges a little. Prick the bottom with a fork. Let it 'seize' in the pre-heated oven for about 5 minutes.

Fill the pie with the prepared mixture of meats and sauce. Have the pastry lid ready rolled out and cut to size. Cut out a small circle in the centre. Wet the edges of the pastry in the tin. Place the lid on top, and pinch the pastry edges together. Roll up a small piece of greaseproof paper to form a chimney and insert into the hole in the middle (this stops the underside of the pastry getting soggy from steam). If you feel artistic, cut shapes in any left-over pastry and stick them on with a little water. Whisk a teaspoon of cold water into the egg yolk and brush the lid with it.

Bake for about 25 to 30 minutes, until the top is golden.

Beef left over from a pot-au-feu is transformed into a comforting dish of stuffed tomatoes

TOMATES FARCIES
STUFFED TOMATOES

This comforting dish is an excellent way to make use of left-over meat. It is usually served with rice.

FOR 4 PEOPLE
**4 large tomatoes
1 thick slice of white bread
a little milk
3 - 4 shallots
1 medium onion
1 clove garlic
60 g (2 oz) butter plus a little extra
250 g (8 oz) left-over meat, minced or chopped
1 large handful of parsley
salt and black pepper
a few dry breadcrumbs, optional**

Preheat the oven to gas mark 6, 400°F, 200°C.

Cut off the tops of the tomatoes. Using a teaspoon, scoop out the insides, being careful not to pierce the skins. Keep the pulp and juice to add to the stuffing.

Cut the crusts off the bread. Soak the bread in the milk.

Peel and chop the shallots, onion and garlic. Cook them in the butter until they soften. Add the meat and cook for a few minutes. (If you are using uncooked sausagemeat it will need to cook for longer, till browned.) Add the tomato pulp and juice. Wash, dry and chop the parsley. Squeeze the milk out of the bread (use your hands - it is the only effective way). Add parsley and bread to the mixture and stir well. Season with salt and pepper. Spoon into the tomatoes. Dot the tops with a little butter. Some people like to sprinkle the tops with dry bread-crumbs. Put the stuffed tomatoes on a gratin dish and into the preheated oven for approximately 30 minutes. (Cooking time depends on the variety of tomato and how ripe they are. They should not collapse.)

VARIATIONS ON CLASSIC DISHES
❖ *The meat can be supplemented or replaced by sausagemeat. Another option is to add a thick slice of ham, minced or chopped.*

POMMES DE TERRE FARCIES BERNARDIN
MONSIEUR BERNARDIN'S STUFFED POTATOES

This is less well-known than stuffed tomatoes but just as delicious.

FOR 4 PEOPLE
**8 medium to large potatoes i.e. 2 per person
1 thick slice of white bread
a little milk
1 large onion
2 cloves of garlic
60 g (2 oz) butter
approximately 250 g (8 oz) left-over meat from a roast,
sauté, stew or pot-au-feu (can be a mixture of meats)
1 handful of fresh parsley
a small glass of white wine
a little vegetable oil
salt and black pepper**

Preheat the oven to gas mark 4, 350°F, 180°C.

Peel the potatoes. Hollow them out lengthways, using a small spoon, leaving a shell roughly 1 cm ($^1/_2$ in) thick. As you finish each one put it into a bowl of water. (Discard the insides, unless you can use them straightaway for a soup.)

Cut the crusts off the bread and soak in the milk.

Peel and finely chop the onion and garlic. Cook them in butter until soft. Chop the meat and the parsley. Squeeze the milk from the bread. Mix the onions, garlic, meat, parsley and bread in a bowl. Add a little glass of wine and a scant tablespoon of oil, salt and black pepper. Stir well.

Drain the potatoes. Sprinkle the insides with a little salt. Fill them with the stuffing. Oil a baking sheet and arrange the stuffed potatoes on it. Bake for 45 to 50 minutes. Lift them onto a serving dish and serve with a fresh tomato sauce (see page 38) poured round them, or serve the sauce separately.

SAUCE TOMATE

FRESH TOMATO SAUCE

This sauce goes well with all sorts of dishes, in particular with the stuffed potatoes (previous page) and the Lafarge's meat loaf.

TO MAKE ABOUT 150 ML (¼ PINT)

1 medium onion
1 clove of garlic
vegetable oil
500 g (1 lb) tomatoes
1 bay leaf
a few sprigs of fresh thyme
a handful of fresh basil leaves
salt and black pepper

Peel and chop the onion and garlic. Cook in a tablespoon of oil until soft. Roughly chop the tomatoes and add to the pan. Add the herbs and simmer, uncovered, for 30 minutes, stirring occasionally. Remove the bay leaf and the sprigs of thyme, and put the rest through a food-mill *(mouli-légumes)*. Taste and season before serving.

BERNADETTE RAVENEAU'S RECIPE FOR CRAPAUDINE

GRATIN OF SLICED POTATOES AND GRUYERE

Bernadette Raveneau serves this with braised beef which makes a substantial meal; it could also accompany a plain roast. It is difficult to get salted back-fat: you may have to persuade your butcher to prepare it specially for you but it is well worth the effort. The dish needs a high temperature to start if off, then a long, slow cooking in a cool oven.

FOR 6 - 8 PEOPLE

1.5 kg (3 lb) firm-fleshed potatoes
(belle de Fontenay type for preference)
500 g (1 lb) salted pork back-fat
500 g (1 lb) grated Gruyère
salt
freshly-ground black pepper

Preheat the oven to gas mark 7, 425°F, 220°C.

Slice the back-fat thinly and use to line a heavy casserole, taking care to cover the bottom and sides completely and reserving some pieces for the top.

Wash, peel, wipe and slice the potatoes, about 0.5 to 1 cm (¼ to ½ in) thick.

Line the bottom of the casserole with the potatoes and sprinkle with Gruyère. Season with salt and pepper. Continue with these two layers, taking care to arrange the slices neatly. Lay the reserved strips of fat on top and start the cooking on the top of the stove - it needs to get really hot.

As soon as the fat at the bottom of the casserole starts to crackle, transfer it to the preheated oven. Continue cooking until the top is golden-brown, then cover the casserole, reduce the heat to about gas mark 2, 300°F, 150°C and continue cooking for 2 to 3 hours. If the top looks in danger of burning, cover the casserole, but remove the lid for the last 30 minutes. It is important to spoon off the fat, which is copious, half-way through the cooking.

VARIATIONS ON CLASSIC DISHES

❖ *The crapaudine can easily be made in large quantities for a party. The amount of fat and cheese used should each be a third of the quantity of the potatoes.*

POTEE BOURGUIGNONNE AND SOUPE AU LARD

Potée bourguignonne differs very little from that of Champagne (see page 132) except that it possibly includes more cuts of salted pork - 'tous de la salaison', emphasizes local cook Christiane Gutigny, listing 'jambonneau, des cottis, une palette du porc, du lard de poitrine' - all of which farmers' wives in the past would have had in their salting jar in the larder, but unfortunately we are unlikely to be able to obtain. It is served with mustard and the little pickled gherkins (cornichons) which accompany most pork charcuterie in France.

To make soupe au lard, the stock from the potée is left to cool overnight. The fat rises and solidifies and is removed easily in the morning. To a litre (1¾ pints) of stock, add two tumblers of water

(200 ml / 7 fl oz) and bring to the boil. Take a loaf of rough bread (not white baguette but an old-fashioned rustic loaf - the local word was 'un jogot', I believe) and slice it up roughly. When the bouillon is really hot, in goes the bread. Add two tablespoons of thick cream and stir. You may add any left-over vegetables from the potée. This old-fashioned peasant soup may not appeal to modern city-dwellers but it was much appreciated by farmers and vignerons, including harvesters, before going to work early in the morning.

Mme Gutigny, herself the wife of a farmer from the Hautes Côtes behind the Côte d'Or, assures me that 'le potage de la Bourgogne est avec du pain' (proper Burgundian soup always has bread in it).

JAMBON AU CHABLIS
HAM IN WHITE WINE SAUCE

This is a useful dish if you have some left-over meat from a cooked joint of ham. It is also used by many French housewives to make a more interesting meal of slices of bought ham. They will buy jambon de Paris cut off the bone. If you are buying ham specially for this dish, try to buy it off the bone as this will have more flavour than pre-packed slices. Use an enamelled saucepan that will not react with the wine in the sauce.

FOR 6 PEOPLE
1 - 2 slices of ham per person (depending on size of the ham and appetite)

FOR THE SAUCE:
**300 ml (½ pint) dry white wine, preferably a Chablis village wine
600 ml (1 pint) well-flavoured chicken stock
500 g (1 lb) fresh tomatoes, diced
6 sprigs tarragon
1 teaspoon tomato purée
salt and freshly ground pepper
300 - 600 ml (½-1 pint) thick cream**

Combine the wine, stock, tomatoes and tarragon in a saucepan. Bring to the boil, cover, then simmer gently for 2 to 3 hours.

Strain, then reduce by boiling hard to about one third of the original amount. Leave to cool a little. Stir in the tomato purée. Taste and season. If it is quite acidic, no matter - the cream is going to balance it.

Add the cream to the sauce and simmer while you warm the ham. To do this, arrange the slices in a dish, pour hot water over them and leave for about 5 minutes. Drain off the water, pour over the sauce and serve.

ESCALOPES DE DINDE A LA CREME

ESCALOPES OF TURKEY BREAST IN A CREAM SAUCE

An economic version of a more extravagant veal dish, this is favourite French family fare, quick and easy to prepare and usually liked by children. It is often served during the harvest, making a change from casseroles simmered in wine.

FOR 6 PEOPLE

250 g (8 oz) mushrooms
60 g (2 oz) butter
2 - 3 shallots
½ tablespoon sunflower or groundnut oil
6 turkey breast escalopes (if cut by your butcher they should be quite thin and weigh about 60 - 90 g (2 - 3 oz) each. If you have to buy the turkey breast in a supermarket and slice it yourself, it will not matter if you end up with smaller pieces - just have more of them)
200 ml (7 fl oz) thick crème fraîche
a squeeze of lemon
salt, pepper and grated nutmeg

Wipe the mushrooms clean and slice thinly. Melt half the butter in a pan and sauté the mushrooms until they are soft and their liquid has almost evaporated. Peel and chop the shallots. Heat the rest of the butter and the oil in a frying pan. When it is hot (but do not let it burn) put in as many escalopes as is convenient at one time without crowding them. When they have browned on both sides, turn the heat down a bit and let them carry on cooking, about another 5 minutes, depending on thickness, until they are cooked through. When they are all cooked, keep them warm on a serving dish.

Sauté the shallots in the same butter. When they are melting, add the *crème fraîche*, stirring and scraping the bottom of the pan. Let it bubble and cook for a few minutes. Add the mushrooms and seasoning including the lemon juice, tasting until you think it is right. Pour over the escalopes and serve.

Good with rice.

COQ AU VIN

CHICKEN IN A RED WINE SAUCE

One is so often disappointed by this in a restaurant that it is easy to forget what a good family dish it is. However, there is really no point in doing this dish with a battery chicken; they have neither the flavour nor the firmness of flesh required.

FOR 6 PEOPLE

1 farm chicken weighing about 2 kg (4 lb)
12 little onions or shallots
150 - 200 g (5 - 7 oz) green streaky bacon in a piece
1 tablespoon butter
1 tablespoon sunflower or groundnut oil
salt and black pepper
1 tablespoon plain flour
100 ml (3½ fl oz) marc de Bourgogne or brandy
1 bottle red Burgundy
a bouquet garni of bay leaf, fresh thyme (or thyme dried on the branch) and parsley
2 cloves garlic
a handful of fresh parsley
250 g (8 oz) button mushrooms, optional
white bread for croûtons

Cut up the chicken so that you have two legs, thighs and wings; cut the carcass with the breasts in two lengthways, or, if you prefer, into four pieces.

Peel the onions or shallots. Remove the rind from the bacon and cut into dice, or lardons. Put the butter and oil in a heavy casserole (such as an enamelled cast-iron Le Creuset) large enough to take the pieces of chicken eventually. Brown the little onions and the lardons. Lift them from the fat and keep on one side. Brown the chicken pieces well on all sides. Season with a little salt and black pepper and sprinkle with the flour, turning the pieces so they are coated.

Warm the glass of *marc* or brandy in a small pan. Pour over the chicken and immediately put a match to it, standing back so that your eyebrows or hair do not catch fire. When the flames have died down, put back the onions and lardons. Pour in the wine. Add the *bouquet garni* and garlic. Bring just to the boil, turn the heat right down, cover and simmer very gently for an hour.

Now is the moment to correct the sauce. Lift out the pieces of chicken, onions, lardons, and keep warm. Discard the herbs and garlic. Boil the sauce to reduce it by about a third. Keep an eye on it for about 20 minutes, checking the taste and consistency. (You aim for a consistency that is neither a thick sauce nor a thin stock and a taste which is intense without being over-powering.) Reunite the ingredients, adding the cleaned button mushrooms if you are using them. Simmer for about ten minutes.

While this is happening, slice the bread, remove the crusts and cut into triangles and fry in a little extra butter or oil.

Serve the *coq au vin* sprinkled with some chopped fresh parsley and with the fried bread triangles arranged round the edge of the dish.

LAPIN DU VERTEMPIERE AU VIN BLANC
RABBIT IN WHITE WINE

Vertempière is the name of the part of Chagny where the rabbits used by Mme de Villaine are raised.

In Burgundy the wine used might be a Bourgogne Aligoté or Bourgogne Blanc, but a Chardonnay from elsewhere could be substituted (but don't tell the Burgundians).

FOR 6 PEOPLE
1 large rabbit, jointed
olive or other vegetable oil
1 medium onion
1 - 2 carrots
2 large tomatoes, peeled
45 - 60 g (1½ - 2 oz) plain flour
½ bottle dry white wine
warm water
2 cloves garlic
bouquet garni of bay leaf, sprigs of
parsley and thyme tied together
fresh tarragon or basil
salt and white pepper
400 g (12 oz) button mushrooms, optional

Brown the pieces of rabbit in a sauté pan in olive or other vegetable oil. While they are browning, peel and chop the onion, carrots and peeled tomatoes into small dice (*mirepoix*). Add them to the rabbit and let them soften. Sprinkle the flour over the meat to act as a thickener for the sauce. Once the meat is well-coated by the flour, add the dry white wine, stirring and deglazing the bottom of the pan. If the pieces of rabbit are not covered, add a little warm water. As the liquid begins to simmer, add the crushed garlic cloves, *bouquet garni*, some of the sprigs of either tarragon or basil, salt, and white pepper. Cover and simmer gently for about 45 minutes stirring occasionally.

If you are using them, wipe the mushrooms clean (leave them whole unless they are big) and add them to the pan for the last 10 to 15 minutes.

Lift the pieces of rabbit onto a serving dish. Check the sauce for seasoning. Remove the garlic and *bouquet garni* and pour over the rabbit. Chop some more fresh tarragon or basil and sprinkle over the top before serving.

MME IMBERT'S BOEUF BOURGUIGNON

MME IMBERT'S BEEF STEWED IN RED WINE

Mme Imbert always serves this during the harvest at the Domaine Leflaive in Puligny Montrachet. As she says, no Burgundian harvest would be complete without it. The bourguignon makes a good party dish (quantities for 25 are given at the end of recipe). Mme Imbert serves this with steamed potatoes and a big green salad, not forgetting the garlic croûtons, which as she says, makes a 'menu complet'.

FOR 6 PEOPLE

1 kg (2 lb) topside beef
125 g (4 oz) green streaky bacon in a piece
1 large onion
2 cloves garlic
a bouquet garni of fresh thyme, parsley, bay leaf
2 cloves garlic
1 bottle of red Burgundy (Bourgogne Rouge
would be suitable)
salt
6 black peppercorns
lard, butter, duck or goose fat for sauté-ing
12 small onions, optional (these are the kind
that are used for pickling and not always available;
shallots can be a good alternative)

FOR THE BEURRE MANIE:

1 teaspoon butter, room temperature
1 teaspoon cornflour (sold in France as Maizena)

FOR THE GARLIC CROUTONS:

French bread
1 clove garlic, peeled and cut in half

'The most important thing,' says Mme Imbert, 'is to prepare the pieces of beef the previous day, marinading them in red wine (preferably a good one), onions stuck with cloves, thyme, bay leaves, a few garlic cloves, and not forgetting the lardons.'

Cut the meat into cubes about 5 cm (2 in) square, trimming off any gristle or extra fat. (French butchers sell suitable cuts as *bourguignon*, already prepared.) Remove the rind from the bacon and dice into lardons. Peel the onion and stick the cloves into it. Peel the cloves of garlic and tie the herbs in a bouquet with string. Put everything into a bowl with the wine, salt and black peppercorns.

The next day drain the beef and lardons, keeping the marinade. Dry the meat, including the lardons, carefully before sautéing in the fat. Brown all sides well. This must be done at a high heat - not a thing to do in your best silk shirt - so that the meat cubes are sealed ready for a long slow cooking. Chop the onion from the marinade and brown. If you are using the little onions, peel and brown them whole. Deglaze the pan with a ladleful of the marinade, scraping the bottom of the pan with a wooden spoon to be sure to incorporate the caramelized juices. Add the rest of the marinade with its herbs and garlic. It should just cover the meat - add water if necessary. Bring to the boil. Let it bubble for a few minutes, then turn down the heat, or remove to a slow oven, and gently simmer, with the lid on, for about 2 to $2\frac{1}{2}$ hours. It must not go too fast or the meat will be stringy and chewy instead of tender. Test the meat with a fork after 2 hours.

Work the flour into the butter in a bowl for the *beurre manié*. At the last minute take a small ladleful of the sauce from the casserole and whisk into the *beurre manié*. When it is incorporated - a matter of seconds - add it all to the sauce and stir it in. Simmer for about 5 minutes until thickened a little.

Cut a slice of French bread per person - grill or bake in the oven - rub with the cut side of the garlic.

QUANTITIES FOR 25 PEOPLE

4 - 5 kg (9 - 10 lb) topside beef
750 g (1½ lb) green streaky bacon in one piece
2 medium onions
3 cloves garlic
3 bottles red Burgundy

Increase the quantity of butter and flour for the *beurre manié* to dessertspoons. Double the number of peppercorns and use a bigger bunch of herbs.

Increase small onions to 25 if you wish, although when this is done in large quantities they are very often replaced by adding the marinade onions, chopped, and browned at the same time as the meat.

When browning the meat, do not put too much in the casserole at one time as it lowers the temperature of the fat, so that instead of browning, the cubes simply stew, which is not what is wanted at this stage. Better to do a few at a time and keep them on one side until all are browned and sealed and ready to cook in the wine.

If you cook the *bourguignon* the day before it is needed, you can remove any fat that has solidified on the surface.

SAUTE DE PORC AU XERES

PORK COOKED IN WHITE WINE AND SHERRY VINEGAR

At Aubert and Pamela de Villaine's Bouzeron estate this is a favourite dish during the harvest. The sherry vinegar works well with the richness of the pork.

FOR 6 PEOPLE

*pork - use leg steaks, one per person, or ask the butcher
for cubed pork for stewing - about 1 kg (2 lb)
1 tablespoon olive oil or sunflower oil
1 medium onion
2 medium carrots
approximately 100 - 125 ml (4 - 5 fl oz) sherry vinegar
approximately 2 teaspoons plain flour
2 cloves garlic
100 ml (3 ½ fl oz) dry white wine
100 ml (3 ½ fl oz) warm water
bouquet garni of bay leaf, sprigs of
parsley and thyme tied together
salt and pepper
fresh parsley for final garnish*

If you are using leg steaks cut them into about three pieces.

Brown the pieces of pork in olive oil or sunflower oil in a sauté pan. Brown them well on all sides. Meanwhile, peel the onion and carrots and cut them into dice (*mirepoix*). Add them to the browned pieces of pork and let them cook in the oil. Once browned add a little of the sherry vinegar to deglaze the bottom of the pan, stirring and dislodging any bits stuck to the bottom. Now add the flour, turning the pork in it so the pieces are coated and the flour begins to brown. Add the crushed clove of garlic, white wine, warm water, *bouquet garni*, salt and pepper and stir. Bring just to the boil and simmer gently with the lid on for about 90 minutes, stirring from time to time.

Lift out the pieces of pork and put into a clean pan. Strain the sauce through a fine conical sieve over the pork. Taste and add some more vinegar until the balance seems right. Bring just to the boil. Correct the seasoning. Serve the pork in its sauce, sprinkled with chopped fresh parsley.

BERNADETTE RAVENEAU'S COURGETTE GRATIN

The Raveneaus' pickers usually have this as an accompaniment to a chicken or meat dish but it also makes a simple and delicious vegetable course on its own.

FOR 4 - 6 PEOPLE

(depending on whether served alone or with a meat dish)

*500 g (1 lb) courgettes
1 tablespoon butter
2 eggs
150 ml (5 fl oz) milk
salt and black pepper
90 g (3 oz) grated cheese (Gruyère, Cheddar
or other hard cheese)*

Preheat the oven to gas mark 4, 350°F, 180°C.

Wash and slice the courgettes. Put them in a saucepan with a very little water to cover the bottom of the pan and a lump of butter (keep some and butter the gratin dish with it). Simmer uncovered until just cooked, about 10 minutes.

Meanwhile, mix together in a bowl large enough to take the courgettes as well, the eggs, milk, salt, pepper and grated cheese, keeping back a little of the cheese. Add the courgettes to the bowl, stir and tip all into the gratin dish. Smooth the top, sprinkle with the remaining cheese, and bake in the preheated oven until the egg mixture has set and the top browned, 15 to 20 minutes.

GENOISE AU COULIS DE FRUIT

SPONGE CAKE WITH A FRESH FRUIT COULIS

Near the de Villaine's vineyards in Bouzeron is a country road where blackberries grow wild. During the harvest, Mme de Villaine picks them to make a coulis to serve with this cake. Some years they ripen too early or too late or other local people get there first, so she substitutes strawberries or raspberries.

You may like to accompany it with a crème Chantilly (sweetened whipped cream). Another way to serve the cake is to cut it in half and fill it with the coulis mixed with some crème Chantilly.

FOR 8 PEOPLE

6 eggs
180 g (6 oz) caster sugar
180 g (6 oz) plain flour
90 g (3 oz) melted, unsalted butter

FOR THE FRUIT COULIS:

250 g (8 oz) soft fruit, such as strawberries, raspberries or blackberries
90 - 125 g (3 - 4 oz) sugar

Preheat the oven to gas mark 4, 350°F, 180°C.

Butter and flour a loose-bottomed or spring clip 20 cm (8 in) cake tin.

Break the eggs into a bowl. Add the sugar and whisk until white and fluffy and the mixture has doubled in volume. You must beat very thoroughly to get air into the mixture (bear in mind that this cake has no baking powder); using a food mixer saves time.

Have a pan of water ready boiling. Take it off the heat, put the bowl over it and continue to beat until it is warm. Now remove the bowl from the pan and continue to beat as it cools. It will thicken a little and when you can see the traces left by the whisk in the mixture, gently but speedily fold in the flour. Finally, fold in the melted butter. Pour into the prepared tin and bake in the preheated oven for 20 to 30 minutes.

After 20 minutes, test with a pointed knife or skewer - if it comes out cleanly, the cake is ready. If not, continue cooking for a few more minutes before testing again. Cool for a few minutes before turning it out of the tin onto a wire rack.

To make the *coulis*, wash the fruit and put into a pan with the sugar. Simmer gently. When the fruit has broken down into a purée put it through a *mouli-légumes* or sieve. Leave to cool.

Pour some of this *coulis* onto a plate, put the cake on top and sprinkle with icing sugar. Serve more *coulis* separately.

POMMES MEURGEY

MARIE-THERESE MEURGEY'S APPLES

This is a nice, homely dish which is even better, says Marie-Thérèse, if you fry the slices of bread or cake a little in butter before preparing the apples.

For each person you need 1 dessert apple and 1 slice of white bread, or sponge cake, or brioche.

Preheat the oven to gas mark 4, 350°F, 180°C. Core the apples but leave them whole. Peel them if you like. If so, you may need to baste with melted butter to prevent them from drying out in the oven.

Butter a gratin dish. Spread the slices of bread or cake with butter and put them in the dish. Arrange the apples, one on top of each slice and bake for about 30 minutes in the preheated oven.

NOELLE LAFARGE'S GATEAU AUX POMMES
NOELLE LAFARGE'S APPLE CAKE

The French are more inclined to serve cakes at the end of a meal than we are - this is very popular with the Lafarge pickers.

FOR 8 PEOPLE
180 g (6 oz) sugar
3 eggs
250 g (8 oz) plain flour
3 teaspoons baking powder
1 tablespoon oil (or equivalent of melted butter)
500 g (1 lb) dessert apples

Preheat the oven to gas mark 7, 425°F, 220°C.

Beat the sugar and eggs together until pale. Sieve the flour and baking powder together, then stir into the egg mixture. Lastly, stir in the oil or melted butter.

Peel and core the apples. Cut into chunks. Incorporate them into the batter. Turn into a bottom-lined and greased 20 cm (8 in) cake tin with a removable base and bake in the preheated oven for 30 minutes.

Serve warm with *crème fraîche*.

VARIATIONS ON CLASSIC DISHES

❖ *For a moister cake, you can separate the eggs and beat the whites until stiff, folding them in once the other batter ingredients have been mixed together.*

❖ *Pears or apricots can be used instead of apples.*

GATEAU ROULE
SWISS ROLL

I vividly remember the sight of Bernadette Raveneau running full pelt across the village street separating her own house and the harvest kitchen, carrying this cake hot from her oven. In order to make enough gâteau roulé for all her pickers to end their supper on a sweet note she was using ovens in both houses. A gâteau roulé cannot wait to be rolled up - it must be done while hot - so she took her life and the Swiss roll tin in her hands (tractors are apt to come round the corner rather fast during the harvest), running like someone in a relay race, to get to the kitchen table where sugared paper and hot jam were waiting. Freshly made and filled with homemade jam, this is certainly worth the run.

MAKES ABOUT 12 SLICES
90 g (3 oz) self-raising flour
3 large eggs
90 g (3 oz) caster sugar plus some extra sugar
3 - 4 tablespoons strawberry, raspberry or other jam

You need a Swiss roll tin measuring 20 x 30 x 1½ cm (8 x 12 x ¾ in) for this. You should line it with parchment baking paper and grease both the tin and the paper.

Preheat the oven to gas mark 7, 425°F, 220°C.

Sift the flour. Take the eggs out of the fridge in good time so that they are at room temperature. Break them into a large bowl. Add the sugar and beat either by hand or using an electric beater. Stop when the mixture is light and fluffy and the whisk leaves a trail when lifted. Now fold in the flour with a metal spoon. Pour the mixture into the tin and smooth the top.

Bake for ten minutes or slightly less - it should be firm when you press it with your finger.

While it is in the oven, gently heat the jam in a pan, just so that it is warm and easy to spread.

Have ready a piece of parchment paper the size of the Swiss roll sprinkled with sugar.

Take the tin out of the oven and turn out the cake onto the sugared paper. Spread the jam. Roll up like a long sausage. Your cake is made. Leave to cool and eat on its own or with icecream or a fruit compote.

R H O N E

$\mathcal{S}$ome of the oldest French vineyards are to be found in the Rhône valley. The Phoenicians and the Greeks are thought to have brought their vines with them as they penetrated up the great river Rhône. Later, the Romans established a colony at Marseilles, almost certainly trading wine for slaves.

◄ *Châteauneuf-du-Pape: the spectacular ruins of the summer palace used by the Popes of Avignon*

The towns of Arles, Nîmes, Orange and Avignon with their Roman remains and great markets, full of colour, are irresistible to the traveller. In the warm air of spring and summer the scent of herbs growing wild on the hills is everywhere. The fishing villages and the little, walled, hill villages just behind the coast with their people, food and wines are evocatively described in Sibylle Bedford's autobiographical novel 'Jigsaw'.

In terms of wine, the region splits naturally into two. In the North, from Vienne to Tain l'Hermitage, mainly red wines from the Syrah grape are grown on the steep, terraced slopes overlooking the river Rhône. These are the deep purple-red coloured Côte Rôtie and Hermitage, made to improve with age. The harvesters have tended to come from the nearby villages and towns and often go home for lunch or bring a picnic to eat in the vines. However there are signs that this is changing, following the lead of the Maison Guigal in Ampuis where they take pride in feeding their pickers.

A small amount of delicious white wine is made from the Viognier grape in Condrieu and several other communes along the river, next to the fruit orchards for which this area is famous.

As the Rhône flows south, the valley spreads out into a rich alluvial plain with hills and *maquis* (scrubland) so typical of this southern landscape. This is a vast production area for red Côtes-du-Rhône and Côtes-du-Rhône Villages from the better placed vineyards. The finest hillside and plâteau sites produce Gigondas, Lirac and, best-known, Châteauneuf-du-Pape.

The spectacular ruin of the summer palace used by the Popes of Avignon after the papal schism of the fourteenth century looks down on the pretty little town of Châteauneuf-du-Pape. The wine of Châteauneauf-du-Pape is traditionally made from 13 different grape types; however, Grenache predominates, (as is the case through-out the Southern Rhône), with Syrah and Mourvèdre of great importance to bring complexity, balance and keeping qualities.

The vineyards are an extraordinary sight because the vines of Châteauneuf-du-Pape appear to grow directly out of a layer of rounded pebbles and rocks smoothed many thousands of years ago on the bed of the Rhône. Somehow their roots find the soil below.

Continuing south, Provence is a useful source of large quantities of rosé and red wines for drinking within a year or two of their harvest. Côtes du Luberon and Côtes du Ventoux are some of the better-known of these wines.

Nearer to the Mediterranean, Rosé de Provence has found a ready market amongst the holiday-makers on the Côte d'Azur. The best red and rosé wine here comes from Bandol, where the Mourvèdre grape gives it individuality.

Much of the picking here has traditionally been done by extended families of North African Arabs, or by Portuguese or Spaniards from across the borders, who bring with them their own cooks and their own preferred cuisine. For this reason dishes, such as *paella* and *couscous*, (widely available, ready cooked, in the markets of the area) have become associated with end-of-harvest celebrations. Increasingly though, grape-picking machines are being used throughout the Rhône valley, and, as someone there said, it does not take much skill to feed a machine.

Gateway to the Clos des Papes vineyard

A welcoming fish stall in Orange market

SAFFRON AND ROSE -
THE COLOURS OF PROVENCE

'When I was a little girl, we used to plant the little corms of the saffron crocus in between the rows of vines. In the autumn we picked the flowers and dried the stamens for fifteen days.' Mme Peyraud, an elderly lady elegantly dressed in a pink dress which is slightly paler than the beautiful Bandol rosé wine of Le Domaine Tempier which she is pouring, is speaking. Brick red when dry, saffron is the essential ingredient in the great fish soups, and the rice dishes of this area, such as *paella*, staining the broth or the rice a glorious yellow and giving them a very special flavour. The rosé wine is the colour of the roofs and much of the dusty-red earth. The use of both the plant and the wine can be traced back to the Phoenicians; saffron and rosé are the colours of Provence.

A motorway carves its way through the scrubland. There are glimpses of the sea; there are medieval fortified villages on hill-tops, then there are the vines growing around Bandol. The Domaine Tempier is to be found near the village of Plan de Castellet.

In 1936 Lucie, known as Lulu, Tempier married Lucien Peyraud. It was during the Second World War, with France under occupation by the Germans, that the couple moved their burgeoning young family from Marseilles to the Domaine Tempier, the house and estate of Lulu's father.

'With seven children I had many mouths to feed,' is how Mme Peyraud explains the origin of her love of cooking. She brushes aside the idea that seven children in ten years could be seen as an impediment to fine cooking.

Both the wines and the food here have an international reputation. The American wine-trader Kermit Lynch writes with affection of the legendary Peyraud family hospitality in his book, *'Adventures on the Wine Route'* (see page 156). Mme Peyraud's

This Domaine is famous for its red and rosé Bandol wines

original and innovative cooking started from a firm base of Provençal traditions and expanded to include recipes and ideas brought back from international travels. It has been a source of inspiration to chefs and writers, including, I believe, Alice Waters, of 'Chez Panisse' in Berkeley, California, who herself has trained and inspired some of the best young chefs of America and Great Britain. The cookery writer Richard Olney is a neighbour and friend of this domaine and his tribute, *'Lulu's Provençal Kitchen'* was published in 1995 (see page 156).

The harvest is a time for traditions, not innovation. 'I like to revive all my old repertoire,' says Mme Peyraud. This estate, which is famous not only for its Rosé but for its fine Bandol Rouge, stopped lodging pickers in 1982 and a few years later Mme Peyraud gave up the cooking for the harvesters. Now they use mainly local families, instead of the students who used to come from other parts of France and farther afield, and for reasons of economy these families prefer to bring and eat a sand-wich at lunchtime, and go home to eat in the evening.

A wide selection of grains and dried pulses on sale in the market

They also use, like many other estates, groups of Arabs (nearby Marseilles has a large population of North African Arabs) who bring their own food. So Mme Peyraud runs through her splendid repertoire of such dishes as *paella* (see page 63), *épaule de mouton aux haricots* (shoulder of mutton with beans, see page 66) and *langue de boeuf pot-au-feu* (boiled tongue, see page 116) for *un noyau*, that is to say some of her family (two sons and daughters-in-law, herself and her husband) and her permanent team of 6 *cavistes* (cellar workers) for the fifteen or so days

of the harvest, usually the last two weeks of September.

However, the final celebratory meal is for all the pickers as well as friends and family. If the harvest is finished in the evening, it takes place the next day at lunchtime; if the last grapes reach the vat-house in the morning, then the party is in the evening.

Time is needed for one of the two great convivial dishes of Provence to be prepared, and, perhaps, for the exhausted harvesters to build up their strength to participate in *la bouillabaise* or *l'aïoli*.

Mme Lulu Peyraud, one of France's great cooks, in her marvellous kitchen

LA BOUILLABAISSE

An exact recipe is a contradiction in terms, it being one of those dishes that depend heavily on what is freshest in the market. Mme Peyraud lists her choice of fish as *rascasse* (a rock-fish from the Bay of Marseilles), *St Pierre* (John Dory), *vivier* (weaver), *tranches de fiéla* (slices of conger eel), *tranches de baudroie* (slices of angler fish), *des crabes* (crabs) and *des moules* (mussels).

'I put all the fish into a big cauldron with potatoes, tomatoes, garlic, fennel (which grows wild here), saffron and water.' A shortish period of fierce boiling follows, and then: 'everyone has a feast of fish in their own soup bowl,' she ends poetically. Alan Davidson's *'Mediterranean Seafood'* (see page 156) is helpful in identifying the fish if you are shopping in the area. In my opinion, those of us without access to the Mediterranean species do better to feast in our imagination than try to replace the flavours of the Mediterranean by those of the Atlantic.

The *bouillabaisse* is accompanied by *la sauce rouille* (a thick, reddish-pinkish mayonnaise). Each diner has a deep soup dish full of fish and broth and is served with garlic *croûtons* (slices of French bread which have been rubbed with garlic, then fried in olive oil or toasted in the oven) and *rouille* to stir into the broth. To make this mayonnaise, Mme Peyraud first makes an *aïoli* sauce by pounding garlic to a paste in a stone pestle and mortar, adding egg yolks and, drop by drop, the fruity, cold-pressed olive oil. Once the sauce is the consistency of a stiff mayonnaise, she adds pounded saffron, red peppers and monkfish livers.

Aïoli is the name of both a sauce and the dish which it accompanies. Accompanies is perhaps the wrong word. The sauce, for many, is the *raison d'être* of the dish, and the dish itself not just a meal but an occasion. The French word *génial* (meaning inspired, having its own genius) seems made for the atmosphere created by this wonderful dish. Properly speaking it is an *aïoli garni* - a garlic mayonnaise, made with the best local olive oil, with boiled salt cod (previously soaked to get rid of the salt), boiled artichokes, beetroots, carrots, potatoes, cauliflower, green beans all served warm - the selection of vegetables is personal but *tout est cuit*. Mme Peyraud includes sweet potatoes, for example, and tomatoes cooked *sur la braise* (on a wood fire). Very often she adds a bowl of *poulpe confit* (octopus, stewed in red wine with onions and garlic). At the end of the harvest, with everyone relaxing round a table outside, *beaucoup de mortiers de sauce* (a good many mortars full of sauce) are happily consumed.

If you want to make an *aïoli* and can get salt cod, allow about 150 g (5 oz) per person. In the markets of Provence two kinds are sold - *morue salée et séchée* is the traditional salted and dried fish, hard as a board, which can be kept for months and must be soaked in water for 48 hours before cooking, and *morue salée*, only salted, which needs soaking for 24 hours. In both cases change the water at least 3 or 4 times during the soaking. Poach the fish in fresh water for about 20 minutes and serve, like the vegetables, warm.

If all the vegetables and fish are to come to the table warm, not over-cooked and at the same time, you need plenty of pots and some extra pairs of hands to drain them at the right moment.

The addition of boiled meat and/or a boiled chicken make this into a *grand aïoli*. Hard-boiled eggs are often included, maybe some soaked and boiled chick peas, and sometimes, cooked snails.

A local person told me she remembers seeing women pickers gathering snails into their aprons as they went through the vines. The snails would then be kept in a cool, dark container and starved to rid them of any impurities, ready to be cooked and added some fifteen to twenty days later, to an *aïoli* or used to make a *cagaoulade*, a very local word for a kind of casserole of snails with little bits of bacon, garlic, local white wine, and in some cases, tomatoes.

Smoked sardines and herrings, salt cod with local olive oil and garlic - typical Provençal products in the market at Orange

HARVEST TEA AT THE DOMAINE DU VIEUX TELEGRAPHE

The reputation of the Domaine du Vieux Télégraphe near Bedarrides is a fine one. The wines, mainly red Châteauneuf-du-Pape and also some excellent white, which is unusual, are shipped to many countries, including the U.S.A and the U.K. For their harvest they need 40 to 50 pickers working for three weeks. They use mainly local people, though some come from farther afield, taking some of their holiday entitlement to work in the vines and earn some extra money. They no longer lodge

The old stone signalling tower from which this domaine takes its name

or feed these workers, but the tradition is to gather everyone together at their farm for a celebratory *goûter* (literally, tea) at the end.

'In my father-in-law's day,' explained Mme Brunier, wife of the proprietor, 'it really was a tea, with a table spread with cakes, fruit tarts and drinks to be eaten as soon as the workers brought in the last grapes. He always asked me to make *des oreillettes*.' This is a local expression

for *bugnes* - sweet, delicious, little fritters eaten warm as soon as they are cooked and lifted from the hot oil in which they are deep-fried, and sprinkled with sugar (see page 67). They are also known locally as *cacho-dents* (teeth-breakers). They are a very popular regional speciality, also made at Christmas and Easter. As someone else told me, here they take the place of the pancakes and waffles, so beloved by the rest of France. They make a delicious partnership with the local, sweet, white muscat wines of Beaumes de Venise.

Now, though they still call it a *goûter*, the Bruniers like to celebrate the end of the harvest with a rather more substantial menu.

This area of Provence is famous for its fine lamb. During the day a fire is prepared outside, and two whole milk-fed lambs (*agneaux de lait*) stuffed with handfuls of thyme which grows wild here, are spit-roasted, and, to give them extra flavour, more herbs are burned on the fire. This must be a mouth-watering sight as the pickers gather for their aperitif.

The first course is usually a selection of salads made from local produce and served in colourful bowls and platters, such as s*alades niçoises* in which bright red tomatoes contrast with the black, small but strong-tasting olives grown nearby, artichoke hearts in oil, roasted red peppers, salads of the local dried pulses (chick peas, white haricot beans or dark brown Puy lentils) all eaten outside, near to where they are produced, while the smell of lamb and herbs perfumes the air.

With the lamb come the French fries or chips, the current passion for which among pickers in all the regions means they are replacing the more old-fashioned regional potato dishes.

Local cheeses - St Marcellin and the little goat cheeses made here - follow and with them, rather charmingly, 'we give everyone a taste of the wine made from the first grapes picked during the harvest,' says Mme Brunier.

'It is not possible every year - it depends on the weather, and of course the wine is not ready (it may still have some *gaz carbonique*, making it a little fizzy) but we think the pickers have a special interest in trying the product of their labours. We pick the Syrah grapes at the beginning of the harvest, so that is what we taste.'

If you have an electric rôtisserie or spit roaster, or a charcoal grill or barbecue and would like to cook a leg of lamb, the essential point is to prepare the lamb by inserting slivers of garlic into the meat and rubbing all over with Provençal herbs and olive oil in advance, so that the flavours may penetrate the meat.

Further south the Teisserenc family, who make Vin de Pays des Côtes de Thongue near Bezier, also have a wonderful lamb dish for the end of harvest celebration.
In this case a flour and water paste hermetically seals a leg of lamb in a cast-iron *cocotte* (casserole) where it cooks very slowly surrounded by fresh figs, walnuts and grapes - all in season locally at the time of the harvest - juniper berries and red wine (see page 61).

Some years, for a change, the Bruniers serve a Provençal *daube* (or casserole) of beef (see page 64). This is also the choice of M. and Mme de Menthon for their celebration at the Château Redortier near Suzette, in the beautiful hills known as Les Dentelles de Montmirail. As Mme de Menthon says - 'A Provençal *daube* with a good

Daube Provençal ready to serve

The cellars at the Domaine du Vieux Télégraphe with wine ageing in jeroboams

bottle of Gigondas - superb!'

High on a hill facing Mont Ventoux, this family has built a *cuverie* and a tasting room where they can receive private customers. Here they are offered the wines to taste before buying and are able to admire the spectacular view at the same time.

The thirty hectares of vines producing Côtes-du-Rhône, Beaumes de Venise and Gigondas - all red wines - are planted higher up than most in the region, with their own micro-climate. The de Menthons are often able to look down into the valley which is shrouded in the thick local fog, while their vines are in sunlight, and in several years they have escaped a frost which devastated the lower properties. Their position also means they harvest late, in October and even, on occasion, in November.

M. de Menthon is a native of the Savoie and it is from this Alpine region that he draws his pickers. Each year many of the same friends return; the majority are ski-instructors or mountain guides, who are happy to earn some money picking grapes in their slack season. They usually cook for themselves, provided with ingredients by the proprietors. But on the final night they gather

together for that local *daube* and excellent Gigondas, which they may have helped to pick in previous years.

To precede the *daube*, Mme de Menthon serves another regional speciality, a *tian* (see page 60), prepared by a friend nearby. The tian takes its name from the shallow, round, earthenware dish in which it is cooked and served. The ingredients may be varied, but it is always similar to a kind of vegetable gratin. Courgettes or spinach are often included, sometimes mixed with eggs or thickened with rice or bread. It is often possible to buy ready-cooked *tians* in the local *charcuteries*. They are usually topped with breadcrumbs and/or grated cheese, and as they come out of the oven golden and bubbling, they look and smell very appetizing. They can also be eaten cold - good outdoor food - and are excellent, hot or cold, accompanied by a fresh tomato sauce. The *tian* at Château Redortier is one of the most robust, a rich mixture of dried haricot (navy) beans and herbs suitable for the cooler autumn weather.

Some of these *tians* - the ones which include eggs and green vegetables - are

Long-lasting red wine from the stony vineyards of Châteauneuf-du-Pape

closely related to the cold omelettes which make such a handy snack and were often made by local pickers for their lunch in the vines (see page 59). Cold omelettes are usually stiff with vegetables and herbs, are not folded in the pan, and, of course, in order to be conveniently portable for a picnic, must not be runny. Local shops sell *gâteau de crespeu* (sometimes spelt *crespeou*), a kind of striped orange and green cake or loaf made up of layers of different cold omelettes, the colours coming from the tomatoes, spinach or herbs used in the omelettes.

The de Menthon's *daube* is followed by local goat cheeses and usually a fruit tart, such as apricot, in which locally-picked fruits are arranged on a pastry base, and, after baking, sprinkled with two tablespoons of Muscat Beaumes de Venise, a white dessert wine, to give them extra succulence (see page 67).

WILD BOAR AND STEEP VINEYARDS IN COTE ROTIE

Wines from the steep slopes near Ampuis

Bernadette Guigal is a harvest enthusiast. She loves the warm and informal atmosphere amongst the eclectic crowd that make up the picking team at the Maison Guigal in Ampuis, near the ancient town of Vienne. Students, unemployed people, professors, doctors all rub shoulders happily - 'c'est très sympa, tout le monde se tutoie.'

Here, more than anywhere, the pickers need the encouragement of hearty meals because the terraced vineyards are so steep that no machines can get into them and everything must be carried on the back. It is hard to appreciate the spectacular view of the river Rhône when struggling not to lose a footing. A fall sends the basket of grapes cascading down the terraces.

The family business was created in 1946. It was already growing in the 1960s and it was then that Bernadette told her mother-in-law that she thought they ought to be feeding all their 25 harvest workers and that she wanted to take on the job.

The number of pickers has more than doubled, as vineyards have been acquired over the years, but the cooking is done with just as much zest. 'The food is relatively simple but varied,' says Mme Guigal. She is a great believer in serving dishes full of calories which give the pickers the energy they need (the expression in French is *les sucre-lents*) - dishes such as gratins of potatoes, or other vegetables, or noodles (see page 61), all with plenty of cream and cheese. A copious second breakfast is eaten in the vines, and at mid-day there are several services of the main meal back at the house - an entrée of a rice salad or quiche will be followed by a good meat dish, usually roasts with one of those delicious and filling gratins and always a dessert, perhaps a fruit salad with a cake from the local pâtisserie.

The evening meal inevitably starts with soup - 'toujours, toujours, la tradition...,' some cold roast meat, always a hot dish, perhaps an omelette with left-over potatoes, simple meals but nourishing after a hard day. Most popular of all are the game dishes, the product of Marcel Guigal's hobby, served at the weekends during the harvest. With dishes like the splendid *civet de sanglier* (marinated wild boar) on the menu, no wonder the Guigals' pickers are prepared to risk life and limb to get the grapes which make the wine that goes into the marinade (see page 65).

Local cheeses in Orange market

Aïoli sauce with warm vegetables - potatoes, artichokes, carrots, beans, chick peas and beetroot

L'AÏOLI

In her description of l'aïoli, Elizabeth David in 'French Provincial Cooking' notes that: 'The magnificent shining gold ointment which is the sauce is often referred to as the beurre de Provence' (Provençal butter). As this suggests, this sauce is stiff, not pourable.

It is made by pounding garlic in a pestle and mortar (using a machine seems to make it taste bitter) to produce a paste, stirring in egg yolks, then, as for a mayonnaise, adding the best possible (cold-pressed virgin) local olive oil, drop by drop at first, stirring all the while.

As for proportions, Elizabeth David suggests 16 cloves of garlic, 3 egg yolks and 500 ml (nearly a pint) of olive oil for eight people. If you are having a larger party, you might like to know that Mme Peyraud uses three heads of garlic to 10 egg yolks for 30 people.

Lemon juice, salt and pepper are used to season to taste at the end. It is not difficult to make but requires one to be unhurried.

In one version a thick slice of day-old bread is soaked in milk, squeezed and incorporated into the garlic paste before adding the eggs and olive oil. Some people think this stabilizes the sauce.

Aïoli is such a good sauce (for garlic lovers) that it is often served with other boiled fish, mixed into soups at the table, mixed into gratins of chick peas or other vegetables, or served with pot-au-feu (see page 32). It is even very good with hard-boiled eggs, or hot potatoes on their own. The Mediterranean diet in which garlic and olive oil are so predominant is now thought to be a factor in the low incidence of heart disease in France and Italy - a good reason to indulge in aïoli whenever possible.

OMELETTE FROIDE AUX POMMES DE TERRE ET PERSIL
COLD POTATO AND PARSLEY OMELETTE

This cold omelette makes a good lunch when served with a green salad, or, packed up, an excellent picnic.

The recipe is adaptable - use more potatoes if you use fewer eggs, it will still work. Potatoes may be peeled or not as you prefer. Dice them and brown them in olive oil. Left-over boiled potatoes could be used up as long as they are not mushy. Add plenty of chopped fresh parsley to the lightly-beaten eggs and season with salt and pepper. Tip them into the frying-pan of potatoes and continue as for an ordinary omelette.

At the point when it would normally be served, this omelette must be turned, using a spatula, or if you're brave, flipped like a pancake, and cooked for a few more minutes. If neither of these methods appeal, you could put your pan under a hot grill for a few minutes instead of turning it. Leave to cool.

The colourful and delicious omelette froide

TIAN OF BEANS

In France red and white haricot beans are sold fresh or semi-dry in the pods, or shelled and dried for the store cupboard. This recipe uses fresh beans but can be adapted for dried ones, by soaking them first overnight and cooking them for longer after the initial soaking in boiling water.

FOR 6 - 8 PEOPLE

250 g (8 oz) white haricot beans
250 g (8 oz) red haricot beans
1 onion
2 carrots
bouquet garni of thyme, parsley and bay leaf,
celery stalk, if liked
250 g (8 oz) salt pork or unsmoked
streaky bacon, in a piece
1 tablespoon lard
salt and freshly ground black pepper
a handful of dry breadcrumbs
approximately 30 g (1 oz) butter

Preheat the oven to gas mark 4, 350°F, 180°C.

Shell a mixture of red and white beans. Soak them in boiling water for 15 minutes. Drain and throw away the water. Start again with fresh water. Bring to the boil in a pan. Put in the beans with a peeled onion, the carrots and the *bouquet garni*. Cover and simmer for 50 minutes.

Prepare the salt pork or bacon. Cut into matchsticks about 0.5 cm ($\frac{1}{4}$ in) wide. Melt a little lard and brown the pork in it.

Drain the beans, reserving some of the liquid. Transfer them and the pork to a gratin dish or other shallow ovenproof dish. Season with salt and pepper and moisten with a little of the reserved stock. If you use dried beans you will need a bit more liquid, about 150 ml ($\frac{1}{4}$ pint).

Sprinkle a layer of breadcrumbs over the top and dot with butter. Bake in the preheated oven for about an hour. The beans should be meltingly soft, the top crisp.

SALADE DE POIS CHICHES
CHICK PEA SALAD

Chick peas like white haricot (navy) beans are grown in Provence and dried for the store cupboard. The smell of the olive oil as it is mixed with the warm chick peas is wonderful. This salad is often served as part of a mixed hors d'oeuvre.

Allow 60 g (2 oz) chick peas per person. Soak the chick peas in water overnight. Drain and put into a pan covered with fresh water. Bring to the boil. Skim off the scum if you are going to continue to cook them in this water. Otherwise, remove from the heat, leave to cool in the water, drain, rinse under cold water, then cook again in fresh water, salted, and with a bundle of herbs, such as bay, thyme and marjoram, added if liked. Some people think chick peas indigestible and hold that it helps to add a pinch of bicarbonate of soda to the first water in which they are boiled.

The chick peas may need two hours slow simmering - test to see if they are soft - it is hard to be exact. Drain, and while warm, dress with olive oil, plenty of salt and freshly ground black pepper and lemon juice to taste. Chopped, mild onion is often added.

GRATIN DE NOUILLES

MACARONI CHEESE

This is the sort of dish so popular during the grape-harvest - filling and energy giving. Similar gratins are made with vegetables such as chard and celery. It is a simple formula which can be adapted.

FOR 4 - 6 PEOPLE
(depending on whether served alone or with a meat dish)

250 g (8 oz) macaroni
100g (3½ oz) grated Gruyère
45 g (1½ oz) butter
200 ml (7 fl oz) crème fraîche
salt, pepper, freshly grated nutmeg

Preheat the oven to gas mark 7, 425°F, 220°C.

Cook the macaroni in a large pot of boiling salted water. Drain thoroughly.

Butter a gratin dish. Put in half the macaroni, half the cheese scattered over them and half the *crème fraîche*. Season with pepper and grate some nutmeg over them. Cover with the remaining macaroni, cheese and *crème fraîche*.

Bake in the hot oven for about 30 minutes, till bubbling and brown on top.

GIGOT D'AGNEAU AUX FIGUES, NOIX ET RAISINS BLANCS

MARIE-PIERRE TEISSERENC'S LEG OF LAMB WITH FIGS, WALNUTS AND GRAPES

A wonderful combination of flavours, this is a dish for early September when fresh walnuts and figs are on sale.

FOR 8 - 10 PEOPLE

1 onion
1 carrot
olive oil
1 leg of lamb, about 2 kg (4 lb)
salt
fresh figs (white or black), about 1 per person
white grapes, about 500 g (1 lb)
fresh walnuts, about 500g (1 lb)
a few juniper berries
2 glasses of red wine
flour and water for the paste

Preheat the oven to gas mark 4, 350°F, 180°C.

Peel and chop the onion and carrot. Heat a little oil in the casserole - choose one which is just big enough for the lamb and for the other ingredients to fit round it. Season the lamb with salt and brown in the oil with the onion and carrot. Turn from time to time so all sides are sealed in the heat - it will take about 20 minutes.

Wash the figs and grapes. Roughly chop the figs. De-pip the grapes, if you so wish. Crack the nut shells and remove the walnuts, peeling off as much of the bitter skins as possible. Chop them roughly. Add all to the casserole round the lamb. Add the juniper berries and the red wine.

While the wine comes to the simmer, prepare a flour and water paste to seal the lid. In a bowl put 500 g (1 lb) plain flour and stir in about 300 ml (10 fl oz) water. As an example, this amount will be enough to seal the lid of a Le Creuset oval casserole size H. Mix to a stiff paste (best done with the hands, a messy but quite pleasant business - a good moment to involve a child). Put the lid on the casserole. Off the heat press the paste all round the edge. Put the lamb into the preheated oven and leave for 2½ hours.

When the time comes to serve the lamb, chip off the hardened paste and be careful to remove it all before opening the lid in case some falls in. Let the lamb rest for 5 or 10 minutes in a warm place before carving it and arranging it with the fruit and nuts and its sauce of red wine and cooking juices in a deep serving dish.

Take-away paella is cooked on the spot in most Provençal markets

MME PEYRAUD'S PAELLA

'There is no typical version,' says Mme Peyraud. Smiling, she adds, 'you can do anything you like in cooking.' How reassuring! Some people seek to mystify; here is one of France's great cooks setting us free to use our heads and sense of taste.

I have suggested using cooked prawns and langoustines because this is what is most widely available here.

Simple to make, this is an adaptable party dish, usually made in large quantities, so amounts are flexible.

**fish - your choice, but Mme Peyraud uses
monkfish because it is firm-fleshed; other firm white
fish would be suitable; cut into bite-sized cubes,
and allow 2 to 3 per person
sea-food - large cooked prawns and/or
langoustines in their shells, one of each per person.
Mussels could also be used, allowing 4 to 6 per person.
(Should be alive when bought - scrub and scrape the
shells to get rid of sand, grit and mud, pull off the
'beards'. Discard any with broken or open shells.
Bring a little water to boil in a large pan, put in
the mussels and with the lid on steam them until they
open, about 5 to 8 minutes.)
meat - 1 chicken leg or thigh per person or
1 - 2 pieces of rabbit per person
rice - 1 rounded tablespoon per person: in
Provence they use a long grain rice grown locally
in the Carmargue area
onions - 1 medium per 6 people
garlic - 2 to 3 cloves per 6 people
tomatoes if liked (not worth including if not really ripe
and full of flavour), 250 - 500 g (½ - 1 lb) per 6 people
a good pinch of powdered saffron
a good pinch of ground aniseed
salt and black pepper
olive oil
boiling water - about twice as much as the
volume of rice**

Take a large frying-pan or shallow sauté pan (unless you have a paella pan) and in it heat enough olive oil to coat the bottom lightly. Brown the pieces of chicken or rabbit and fish. Brown the peeled, chopped onion and garlic. Peel and chop the tomatoes, if using them, and sauté for a few minutes in the pan.

Cover all these ingredients with boiling water. Add the saffron (and make sure when you buy it that it is a good saffron and not a substitute), aniseed, salt and pepper. Add 1 table-spoon of rice per person. Stir, turn down the heat and simmer gently for about 20 minutes. The rice should absorb the water in that time.

Taste and if you feel the rice is still not quite cooked add a little more hot water and continue cooking for a few minutes.

Towards the end of the cooking add the prawns, langoustines and mussels, all in their shells, to heat through. The colours and flavours of this dish are most enticing.

Plentiful olives and olive oil at a local market stall

DAUBE PROVENÇALE

This recipe is based on the one used by Mme Brunier from 'La Cuisine Provençale' by J. B. Rebouil, thought of locally as the cooking Bible.

What makes a daube, a daube? This dish, which crops up on almost all harvest menus, is perfect for feeding a large party. Preparations must be made in advance, and all authorities seem to agree that the flavours improve and develop on reheating, which makes it convenient. Is there a definitive version? Surely not. Everyone who makes it has a favourite recipe, from which over years they may have deviated without noticing. The use of local wine, orange zest for seasoning (only a small thing but the taste comes through subtly) and spices such as cloves, juniper berries and all-spice, make this version Provençale, but there are many other versions.

Many recipes start by frying diced streaky bacon, and in some the meat is larded with little bits of bacon fat. Tastes have moved away from dishes with a lot of fat; meat is being produced with as little fat as possible now, but it is important for the meat in these dishes requiring long, slow cooking to have some fat, otherwise it will become dry and stringy, instead of soft and melting.

There are two points worth noting. The first concerns the wine for the marinade, and ultimately for the cooking: the better the quality, the better the end result. The ladies of whom I am writing have the advantage that good wine is always available to them. But for us who have to buy our cooking wine, it is better to save money by buying cheaper cuts of meat than poor quality wine. The truth is that industrialized, mass-produced bottles of neutral wine result in thin, unpleasant sauces. Naturally this does not mean that you must buy a First Growth for your daube, just that it is better not to cook with anything you would not be happy to drink.

The second point concerns the browning of the meat (and this applies whether a recipe calls for meat in one piece or diced). All the French women I have watched making this kind of dish have insisted that this step is vitally important to the success of the dish, and not just because browned meat looks more appetizing. They get whatever fat or oil they are using smoking hot; they themselves get very hot, and probably spattered with fat doing it, but consider it worth it.

The technical reasons are well described in some detail in Part 1 of the translated edition of Escoffier's 'Guide Culinaire' (see page 156), for those who would like to understand the process better. But, in essence, this searing of the meat allows the long cooking to soften the fibres gradually without ruining the texture of the meat.

The only other thing to say is that making a daube is not difficult, but it does need care and attention to detail - the result is a dish of wonderful flavours.

FOR 8 PEOPLE
**2 kg (4 lb) stewing beef - cuts with
some fat, such as top rump, or silverside or even
brisket (U.K.) or a boneless pot roast, such as chuck
underblade (U.S.A.) are suitable
7 oz (200 g) pork fat or 125 g (4 oz) lard
1 onion, roughly chopped
4 - 5 cloves garlic
a piece of orange zest**

FOR THE MARINADE:
**2 onions, cut in quarters,
2 - 3 carrots, peeled and roughly chopped
a bouquet garni (bay leaf, thyme and parsley tied in a
little bunch, with a stick of celery if liked)
salt, peppercorns and other spices (4 - 5 juniper berries,
2 - 3 cloves, 4 - 5 allspice berries)
1 bottle red wine (here Côtes-du-Rhône
would probably be used)
1 small glass red wine vinegar**

Cut up the meat into cubes weighing about 125 g (4 oz) each. Put them with the marinade ingredients into a bowl and leave for 6 hours in a cool place, or overnight in the refrigerator.

Drain the meat and vegetables, reserving the liquid. Place the liquid in a pan and boil hard to reduce by half. Skim off any scum as it boils.

Dry the pieces of meat carefully. This is important as they will not brown successfully if wet.

Melt the fat in a pan. If using pork fat, lift out any resulting little balls of frizzled fat which have not melted, using a skimmer. Brown the onion gently in the fat and set aside.

Let the fat get very hot and brown the pieces of meat well on both sides in batches. You may find it easier to do this in a heavy-based frying-pan, transferring the meat to a casserole

RHONE

once browned. Add a little of the marinade to the caramelized juices in the pan, stir and pour into the casserole. (An enamelled cast-iron casserole is ideal.)

Add 4 or 5 cloves of garlic, the orange zest, and the vegetables, herbs and spices from the marinade. Pour over the reduced marinade, adding a cup of warm water. The meat should not be completely drowned. Cover with foil and the casserole lid and simmer very gently for 4 to 5 hours. Timing depends on the cut of meat used; it is best to check after $3\frac{1}{2}$ hours. Baste the top of the meat with the liquid from time to time, so that it does not dry out if it is not quite covered. Remove any fat before serving - this is much easier to do if the *daube* is allowed to cool so that the fat rises to the top and can

be spooned off; it can be reheated when needed. You may also like to remove the orange peel and *bouquet garni*.

Mme Brunier says the *daube* should be served very hot and goes well with boiled potatoes or fresh pasta. She adds black olives towards the end of the cooking.

VARIATIONS ON CLASSIC DISHES
❖ *Many cooks thicken the sauce. After browning the meat, sprinkle with a little flour and cook briefly before adding the marinade. Or add a beurre manié (see page 31) just before the end of the cooking. If you prefer a sauce with more body but do not wish to add flour, you could drain it from the meat and reduce it a little by boiling in an open pan, before reuniting with the dish and serving.*

CIVET DE SANGLIER
MARINATED WILD BOAR OR LEG OF PORK

Mme Guigal marinates gigots (legs) of wild boar in some of their own excellent Côte Rôtie with salt, pepper, cloves, thyme, bay leaves, onion, garlic, carrots, a little olive oil and cognac for 48 hours. While the meat is roasting she reduces the marinade to make a sauce. As she points out, the longer wine cooks, the more its natural acidity predominates. This is corrected by adding some redcurrant jelly and a little cream at the end.

The following recipe is an adaptation to use with leg of pork. It works well, and the sauce, a glowing dark red, is deliciously winey.

FOR 10 - 12 PEOPLE
half a leg of pork, weighing about 3 kg (6 lb), rind removed

FOR THE MARINADE:
1 onion, stuck with 3 or 4 cloves
2 - 3 carrots, roughly chopped
2 bottles red wine (the Guigals can use Côte Rôtie, or Côte du Rhône but this is expensive. Alternatively, a wine from the Midi such as a Vin de Pays d'Oc, or indeed a Shiraz from Australia would give a good result)
2 - 3 cloves of garlic
2 bay leaves
bunch of fresh or dried thyme sprigs
2 tablespoons olive oil
2 - 3 tablespoons cognac
salt
6 black peppercorns

FOR THE SAUCE:
1 teaspoon of cornflour
approximately 1 tablespoon redcurrant jelly
4 - 5 tablespoons pouring cream
salt and black pepper

Place the marinade ingredients and the pork in a large bowl. Leave it somewhere cool for 48 hours. If you have to put it in the fridge, allow a day longer.

When you come to cook it, have the oven preheated to gas mark 4, 350°F, 180°C.

Lift the pork from the marinade, drain and put it straight into a baking tin and into the oven. Roast for 30 to 35 minutes per half kilo (1 lb), in this case about 3 hours.

To make the sauce, sieve the marinade into a pan - avoid aluminium which will react with the wine. Boil the liquid, uncovered, to reduce it by about half, skimming off the rather unappetizing looking scum that comes to the top. Allow about 20 to 30 minutes for this.

Put a teaspoon of cornflour in a little bowl, add a small ladle of the reduced marinade and mix until smooth. Add this to the pan and let it simmer, stirring for about five minutes.

Taste. Stir in half the redcurrant jelly, then taste again. Add the rest of the redcurrant if needed. Add the cream. Taste once more and add salt and pepper as you think fit.

While you are working on the sauce, take the pork out of the oven and let it rest for a few minutes. Carve and arrange on a dish. Pour the sauce over it and serve.

EPAULE D'AGNEAU AUX HARICOTS

SHOULDER OF LAMB WITH DRIED HARICOT BEANS

Although originally made with mutton this works well with lamb. The shoulder is braised in a heavy, covered casserole, with carrots, onions, wine, stock, garlic and herbs. Dried haricot beans are partly cooked, then added to the casserole towards the end of the cooking, taking on the mingled flavours of the other ingredients and becoming soft and melting.

The French would serve this as it is without any other vegetables.

FOR 8 PEOPLE

1 shoulder of lamb, weighing about 2 ½ kg (5 lb)
a little olive oil
2 large carrots
2 medium onions
approximately 250 ml (8 fl oz) local red wine
(Côtes de Rhône for example)
salt and pepper
2 large cloves of garlic
1 bay leaf
1 teaspoon of dried thyme, or a small bunch
of fresh thyme
1 tablespoon of tomato paste
600 ml (1 pint) stock (chicken is suitable)
500g (1 lb) dried haricot beans

The day before: wash the beans, pick out any stones, and soak overnight.

Preheat the oven to gas mark 4, 350°F, 180°C.

Trim off any extra fat on the meat. Heat the olive oil in the casserole (which should be just big enough for the meat and vegetables round it). When it is hot, brown the meat, turning from time to time for about 20 minutes.

Meanwhile, prepare the carrots and onions by peeling and slicing them.

Remove the lamb to a dish. Brown the vegetables in the oil for a few minutes, stirring them so that they do not burn. Remove them to the dish. If there is a lot of oil, or the lamb has produced a lot of fat, pour it off - or, off the heat, wipe the casserole with kitchen paper. Now, back on the heat, deglaze the pan with the wine, stirring at first to dislodge any bits from the meat or vegetables, then let it boil to reduce by about half.

Season the lamb with salt and freshly ground black pepper.

Add the lamb and vegetables to the wine. Peel the garlic and gently crush under the wide blade of a knife. Add the garlic, bay leaf, thyme and tomato paste to the casserole. Add stock till it comes about half-way up the lamb. Let it simmer gently for a few minutes, cover with foil and the lid and move to the oven. Cooking time is about 2½ hours, but after about half an hour check to see if it is cooking too fast - it should only simmer gently - and turn down the heat if necessary. Take the opportunity to spoon some of the liquid over the meat.
Do the same when you add the partly-cooked beans, after a further 1½ hours.

To cook the beans, drain them, put into a saucepan and cover with cold water (no salt). Bring to the boil. White scum will be produced and can be skimmed off. Reduce the heat, cover and simmer for 45 to 60 minutes. It is difficult to be accurate about the timing; if they are old they may need a bit longer. They should be just slightly undercooked at this stage. Leave them in their cooking water until you are ready to drain and add them to the casserole for the final half hour of cooking round the lamb in the oven.

To serve, carve the lamb, arrange it with the beans and braising vegetables on a dish and pour over some of the cooking liquid.

OREILLETTES

SWEET CRISP FRITTERS

The oreillettes should be eaten as soon as possible. They do not keep, but then there are rarely any left to keep.

500 g (1 lb) plain flour
4 egg yolks
150 g (5 oz) caster sugar
2 teaspoons orange-flower water
100 ml (3½ fl oz) water
approximately 60 - 125 g (2 - 4 oz) unsalted
butter, as liked, melted and cooled
oil for deep-frying

Sieve the flour onto a pastry-board. Make a well in the centre and put in the egg yolks, sugar, orange-flower water and water. At this point you can add some melted butter. Mix into a dough and leave to rest for an hour or two.

Divide into pieces weighing approximately 60 g (2 oz) each. Working with one piece at a time, roll out on a floured surface, to a thickness of barely 2 mm (¹/₁₂ in). Using a pastry-wheel, cut diagonally to make four or five ribbons. Traditionally these are formed into a ring shape but Mme Brunier does not do this.

The final stage requires a deep-fryer of hot oil. Tip in the ribbons in batches. As soon as they turn golden-brown, lift out with a slotted spoon and sprinkle with sugar.

TARTE AUX ABRICOTS ARROSEE
DE MUSCAT BEAUMES DE VENISE

APRICOT TART MOISTENED WITH MUSCAT BEAUMES DE VENISE

This lovely tart is served at Château Redortier - both the fruit and the wine are local - at the end of harvest celebration meal.

FOR 6 - 8 PEOPLE

FOR THE SWEET SHORTCRUST PASTRY
(to fill a 25 cm (10 in) tart tin):

200 g (7 oz) plain flour
1 small pinch of salt
about 15 g (1 oz) caster sugar
100 g (3½ oz) butter at room temperature
1 egg
a little water

FOR THE FILLING:

750 g - 1 kg (1½ - 2 lb) ripe apricots
1 tablespoon sugar, optional
2 - 3 tablespoons Muscat Beaumes de Venise
(keep the rest of the bottle to drink with the tart)
1 egg yolk, optional

Preheat the oven to gas mark 6, 400°F, 200°C, with a heavy baking sheet on the middle shelf.

Sift the flour into a large bowl with the salt and sugar. Roughly cut up the butter, then with the tips of your fingers, speedily rub it into the flour until it looks like breadcrumbs.

Lightly beat the egg with about a teaspoon of cold water. Make a dip in the middle of the heap of flour, pour in the egg and mix until it is a supple and moist paste. Form this into a ball, cover and leave to rest for an hour.

Butter a 25 cm (10 in) removable-base, fluted tart tin. Roll out the pastry on a floured surface and line the tart tin with it. Chill for 1 hour.

Cover the pastry with a piece of buttered baking parchment, weighted with dried beans. Put into the preheated oven on the baking sheet for about 8 minutes. Remove the paper and beans. Prick the base of the pastry with a fork and return to the oven for about 3 minutes more. It should be just starting to come away from the sides of the tin; do not let it get too brown.

Reduce the oven heat to gas mark 4, 350°F, 180°C.

Stone the fruit and slice thinly. If they are under-ripe, it might be worth poaching the slices for a few minutes in a little water and sugar but you must drain them carefully.

Arrange them in concentric circles in the pastry shell. In order to prevent the pastry becoming soggy, many people like to brush the base with egg yolk before doing this. Sprinkle the fruit with the tablespoon of sugar if using.

Bake in the preheated oven for about 20 minutes. This tart is nice served warm, but whether eaten warm or cold, sprinkle the fruit with the Muscat Beaumes de Venise just before serving. It should make a sensational finish to the meal.

BORDEAUX

If you have heard of wine, you have heard of Bordeaux. And with the word Bordeaux a picture of a château comes to mind. After all, as the many tourists will tell you as they get off their state-of-the-art coach to worship at the shrine of a world-renowned château, it is 'very famous'.

◄ *Chais (cellars) at Château Magdelaine, St Emilion*

*B*ordeaux is also the very bastion of British snobbism about wine. The British even have their own name for the red wines: claret. White, male, upper-class, public-school-educated members of the wine trade are most at home here. The fact that the Earl of Shrewsbury allowed himself to be defeated by the French in 1453 - thereby losing the territory that Eleanor of Aquitaine had brought to the English crown by her marriage to Henry II in 1152 - has not, in the long term, weakened the trading connection.

Bordeaux is a great city, the most sophisticated wine capital in France. The old town near the river dates principally from the seventeenth and eighteenth centuries. The magnificent architecture of the quays alongside the Gironde reflects the commercial confidence of that era. It is still a busy port. In the city centre it is a pleasure to stroll down the elegant Allées de Tourny and to sit in a glassed-in pavement *brasserie*, eating local oysters and *omelette aux cèpes* (wild mushroom omelette). The opera house is across the street; posters advertise plays, concerts or a new exhibition at one of the museums. A short walk away some of the best food produce in the world can be bought (not cheaply, of course) in and around the modern, covered market, Le Marché des Grands Hommes. Vegetables and fruit from nearby Spain, an astonishing array of fish and seafood from the Atlantic, the best meat, all the most luxurious products of Périgord, such as *foie gras* and *confit d'oie*; specialist cheese shops - among the cheeses from all over France it is a surprise to find the big round balls of aged Dutch Gouda which are a speciality here; and shops where they have perfected the art of hand-making chocolates. The citizens of Bordeaux can eat, as well as drink, like kings.

Access to the Atlantic meant that the Bordelais were exporting wines many years before land-locked regions, such as Burgundy. But the Bordeaux merchants have had their downs as well as their ups. Towards the end of the nineteenth century the phylloxera, a louse which attacks the roots and ultimately kills the vines, was responsible for enormous damage (in other areas too), with all the financial implications from the subsequent uprooting of the vineyards and the re-planting with resistant stock from America, where the louse originated. Vines take at least four years to produce a crop and many years to reach maturity. Although most farmers are natural grumblers, this really was a devastating set-back.

In 1956 frost killed many of the vines. Again there had to be re-planting.

More recently, in 1973, the Bordeaux market collapsed spectacularly. There had been two boom years when there hardly seemed enough wine to satisfy the market, despite the huge production of the area. Prices soared for the great vintages, then high prices began to be asked, and paid, for the poor vintages. Speculators came into the market - wines were being bought and sold for huge prices, not for drinking but as an international

One of the Janoueix properties, Château le Castelot

commodity. You might think it would be easy to see this must end in tears, but the atmosphere at that time was a frenetic and heady one. Then came the oil crisis and economic recession. The bottom dropped out of the market. Merchants were left holding large stocks of wine no-one seemed to want. Some went under, and most took years to recover from the financial disaster.

The vineyard of Les Grandes Murailles, St Emilion

Bordeaux is the most important area on the globe for the production of the full range of table wine styles. There are dry white wines ranging from cheap to expensive and the famous sweet dessert white wines of Sauternes and Barsac. Among the reds there is everyday-drinking plonk which sells at reasonable prices, a broad spectrum of mid-price, high quality wine, and, of course, the very finest bottles from the world famous châteaux.

All through the eighties, the spread of wine-making skills in the area resulted in much greater production of high quality wines. More people were studying oenology, the science of wine-making, at the University of Bordeaux in Talence, as indeed they were at the University of Dijon in Burgundy. Professors Peynaud and Ribereau-Gayon, indefatigable in their pursuit of quality, were signed up as wine-making consultants to dozens of leading properties. Fine wine from Bordeaux is no longer rare, but even so, the well-known châteaux have stayed consistently expensive. Other parts of the world have planted the

classic Bordeaux vine types and universities in America and Australia are also producing good oenologists; a new, well-informed wine-drinking public is willing to experiment. Perhaps Bordeaux is no longer in a position to be complacent.

The wine area known as Bordeaux is extremely large and is made up of a number of distinct vineyard areas, each with its own character derived from the different soils and micro-climates. When you realise that it is at least 120 miles from the tip of the Médoc, situated on the peninsular north of the city, to the Sauternes and Barsac vineyards in the south, you understand the scale of the place. It is also understandable that several different grape types are planted to suit the different conditions. Some wines are made from a blend of different vines planted in the same vineyard.

The Sauvignon Blanc is a grape which brings fruitiness to the dry whites, but the classic white Bordeaux grape is the Semillon, which produces a rich, broad-flavoured wine that ages well. When climatic conditions are right, Semillon is attacked by 'noble rot', which has the benign effect of concentrating the sugar in the fruit and results in the production of luscious dessert wines.

There are three main red grape types. The first is the Cabernet Sauvignon. It gives deep purple-red wine with its own intense character and relatively strong tannins. It is the backbone of the character of the wines of the Médoc and gives them their legendary ageing ability. Equally important is the Merlot which produces a more supple, very ripe wine and is widely planted in all the regional *appellations*, such as Côtes de Castillon, Côtes de Bourg and Premières Côtes de Bordeaux. Merlot is also the grape which gives fleshiness and flavour to the best wines of Pomerol and Fronsac. Thirdly, there is the Cabernet Franc, which is particularly planted around St Emilion. It is this grape which, when vinified with the Merlot, can produce superbly balanced wines suitable to be enjoyed while young, as well as ageing elegantly.

There is a bewildering number of châteaux (and the word 'château' covers a variety of different buildings, by no means all of them on a grand scale, and some of them

Filling magnums of vin ordinaire for the pickers' lunch at Château Haut Sarpe

uninhabited). In 1855 the first major classification of some of the best châteaux was made. In the Médoc, the villages of Margaux, St Julien, Pauillac and St Estephe were covered, and for the dessert wines, Sauternes and Barsac. At the top there were four: Lafite, Latour, Margaux and one outsider: Haut Brion in the Graves area was judged to be so exceptional that it had to be included in this select band of First Growths. Château d'Yquem headed the classification in Sauternes. Much later, in 1973, Mouton Rothschild was elevated to the First Growths.

St Emilion had to wait a hundred years to be classified, Cheval Blanc and Ausone being recognised as First Great Growths. Some outstanding areas have never been classified, for instance, Canon Fronsac and Pomerol, but in the latter it has long been acknowledged that Pétrus is on the same level as the Médoc First Growths.

Many of the lesser known areas, where they are now making the best value wines of all, are completely uncharted waters. It is difficult to make sense of all this - with the result that it has kept many experts in business for years!

Numbers used to allocate rows to the pickers and a demi-john for refreshment

HARVEST RITES

It is autumn and it is misty; easy to miss a turning in this unsigned country, where little roads criss-cross between large vineyards. Leaving behind the suburbs of the market town of Libourne on the banks of the wide Dordogne river, villages are not much more than a cluster of buildings around a crossroads. Sometimes one glimpses a small château behind a stand of trees. The impression is that vines are more important than houses here.

Driving at dusk down a straight country road in Pomerol a strange sight meets the eyes. A bonfire is blazing. As the flames die down, a team of sturdy women approach it, carrying a large contraption on long poles. Like high-priestesses in a pagan ritual, they lower it onto the embers, then stand back. In the falling light, figures are emerging from the anonymous farm buildings on either side of the road, to stand around the fire. The ladies advance again, in formation. They lift the contraption off the fire, and, wielding forks, fall on the sausages grilling on it to turn them. A delicious smell from the

burning dried vine shoots and grilling meat wafts across the courtyard encouraging the pickers to hurry in to dinner. On the other side of the little road, on neatly raked gravel, an evening game of *boules* has just finished in front of the rather dull grey building where the pickers are lodged adjoining the *chais*. This is the great, though architecturally unpretentious, Château Pétrus.

In the kitchen the cooks are bringing in the sausages ready to serve them with *flageolets verts* (small pale-green dried beans) after the soup. Trays of the dessert, *oeufs au lait* (see page 93), made earlier, are waiting. The 150-strong team of pickers here have already harvested the prestigious vineyard of Pétrus, La Fleur Pétrus, (this is where the kitchen is) and most of the other properties in Fronsac, St Emilion and Pomerol owned by the family business, J-P. Moueix.

Coaches are unloading tourists in well-organized car-parks on the outskirts of the pretty, historic little town of St Emilion. 'La Grande Muraille', a large wall - the

Barbecued brochettes on a grand scale

ruined remains of the church of the Jacobins - with a small vineyard in front of it, is being photographed again. In the Restaurant Francis Goullée, on the corner of a narrow street, Mme Goullée is in calm control, awaiting her lunchtime clients. Her chef-husband is in the kitchen. She is just the sort of front-of-house professional who inspires confidence in the diner; it is obvious that in her hands all will run smoothly.

In the autumn, Mme Goullée takes three weeks off, not, as you might imagine, to put her feet up, but to run the kitchen for the Moueix's harvesters. 'The harvest - you cannot imagine with what tenderness I think of it - it is my holiday! I am a different person then,' she says, standing at the door of the restaurant, not a hair out of place and immaculately dressed.

As she drives a blue Deux-Chevaux van at speed up a dirt track between vines to bring a second breakfast to the workers, she is dressed in a track suit. Here she is Annie, not Mme Goullée. Handing out hot coffee and croissants, and cracking jokes with old friends among the team, she feels she can be her real self.

Yet that real self is still a stickler for good organization, however much she regards this as a holiday. She has a team of three cooks and five helpers to prepare vegetables, serve the meals and wash up. These are all local women, who know each other well and who work in the vines during the rest of the year. The menus are planned well in advance, the ingredients ordered (100 kilos of potatoes a day, 50 kilos each of carrots and onions - these are the sort of quantities needed), schedules made and rigorously adhered to in the hurly-burly of the harvest kitchen. 'The Moueix's put anything I want at my disposal,' she says, adding with some pride, 'all the pickers put on weight!'

As she says, there are rituals: thick soups for lunch; clear *consommés* for dinner; every Saturday a *pot-au-feu* at mid-day; Wednesdays *la poule à la crème* with rice; Friday lunch is *hachis Parmentier* (made from left-over meat scrupulously saved - 'it simply cannot be made from fresh meat,' (see page 88); Friday night is omelette night;

casseroles like *blanquette de veau* (see page 85) are for lunch; roasts or grills in the evening; always a homemade dessert for dinner; and fruit and yogurt at mid-day, except on Sundays, when there are sorbets.

In the vines of La Fleur Gazin, the swallows appear to be dive-bombing the pickers as they swoop low over the vines, eating little insects stirred up as the leaves are parted. Just before mid-day the last grapes of the harvest are loaded onto the tractor, which is decorated with a bunch of flowers. There are squeals and shouts as one or two pickers are set upon, dragged to the truck and thrown into the sticky mass - you get the feeling some scores are being settled. A large jar of wine is passed round and the *Chef du Culture* sets off a rocket to signal the end of the work. It is time for lunch and a hard-earned break before the celebration dinner.

The bundles of dry vine shoots are piled high outside the kitchen door. The cooks are arranging an impressive number of *magrets de canard* (duck breasts) on the grill. The atmosphere is convivial - last games of *boules* are being played, cars and trucks moved to make way for a fireworks display, a local band is setting up in the refectory and the cooks' helpers are arranging posies of flowers in jam-jars, jugs, or anything else to hand, to make the tables festive.

Christian Moueix, sitting at the head of one of the tables, is surrounded by his team of Oenologist, *Chef du Culture*, *Maître de Chai*, *Régisseur* and Export Director, all of whom will respond to chanted requests for a song as the night wears on and the wine flows. But now, before the inevitable soup - which today will be followed by *bouchées à la reine* (flaky pastry *vol-au-vents* filled with seafood in a creamy sauce) before the duck breasts - grilled over vine shoots - the band strikes up a fanfare, and in comes a delegation of the pickers with bouquets of flowers for the owner and the cooks.

From the *gerbe* or sheaf of flowers, traditionally offered by the workers to the owners at the end of the harvest, comes the Bordelais name for the celebration, *gerbebaude*. Château La Fleur St Emilion Grand Cru has been

Magrets de canard ready to grill on a fire of vine shoots at La Fleur Pétrus ➤

succeeded by the Pomerol Château Lagrange, and now
with the rhum babas (as Mme Goullée puts it, her
husband has 'intervened' to make the *vol-au-vents* and the
desserts), a sparkling wine is being poured. There are
three pickers with birthdays, so their desserts come with a
candle, a round of 'Happy Birthday to You', a good many
kisses and toasts. The singing starts in real earnest, only
interrupted by a speech of thanks from Christian, then it
is time for silly party games and energetic, uninhibited
dancing until the early hours of the morning.

The next day the room will seem empty, half of it
curtained off, when the *cuverie* workers, *stagiaires* (young
people in training) and other personnel come into lunch.
Some lingering goodbyes have been said, and harvest
romances may blossom or wither; many renew friend-
ships year after year as they return, leaving their normal
work as train-drivers, bank clerks, electricians, or teachers
- it's a diverse crowd. The students will move on, trying to
get work at other châteaux while there is still money to be
earned. There are usually some young English and
Americans - the experience they have just had has been
unique. Château Pétrus may be the smallest and rarest of
the great First Growths but the 'picking family' in which
they have been made welcome is unstuffy, hard-working
and fun.

Do things taste better grilled over Cabernet or Merlot
vine shoots? This esoteric question has little relevance in
most of our lives, but here in the Bordeaux region it can
generate a lively debate since there are vine shoots
(*sarments*) in abundance, kept from the time of pruning.
The flavour they impart to meat or fish is delicious and
during the harvest some of the best meals are of sausages,
brochettes (cubes of veal or lamb interspersed with bacon
on skewers), fresh sardines, pork chops, or thin slices of
pork breast known as *du lard* or *ventreche*, all grilled
sur sarments. It is typically local.

Some of the older dishes have gone out of fashion.
Mme Gaudrie of Château Villars (where they have used
a machine to harvest since 1981) describes a cod dish
which used to be served on Fridays according to religious
custom. A large piece of cod is boiled in water with

A shrine for lovers of the Merlot grape - the approach to the cellars

potatoes. When cooked, most of it is made into *morue en
salade* (also known as *brandade de morue*) - it is mashed with
a fork, with some of the potatoes, a lot of garlic and parsley and some olive oil, salt and pepper, then eaten cold.
The cooking broth, together with the remaining cod and
potatoes, is poured over slices of day-old bread, with
some slices of garlic browned in butter or oil and parsley,
and eaten as a soup. Peasant dishes like this are no longer
much appreciated.

Many châteaux continue to use traditional cooking
methods. At Château Figeac, for instance, they use huge
old cauldrons over wood fires for their soups and for
pot-au-feu. This lovely property, which is a *Premier Grand
Cru Classé* in the St Emilion area, is renowned not only for
its wine but also for its spectacular *gerbebaude*. There are
games and sports and one famous year there were circus
people amongst the harvesters, who did trapeze acts in
the courtyard. A band of gypsies, who return each year to
pick the grapes, perform traditional dances.

GOOD FOOD AND THE
BEST NIGHT-CLUB IN TOWN

A tantalizing smell of grilling meat leads to a charming room across a little garden. Mme Chabrerie has worked at Château Haut Sarpe for 22 years and her husband is *Chef de Culture*. This morning she is grilling steaks - huge pieces of meat from cattle raised on the farm (two cows are killed for the harvest) over vine shoots in a renaissance fireplace. On cold evenings the harvesters come in here to warm up with *vin chaud* (hot wine, with sugar and spices, see page 93) and roast chestnuts on the fire. Up some wooden stairs is one of Jean Janoueix's many antique collections, this one of old cooperage implements. Mme Chabrerie sprinkles chopped shallots over each batch of steak (*entrecôte à la bordelaise*, see page 79), as she takes them off the fire. It is hot work and she must be glad of a breath of fresh air as she walks back across the garden to the harvest kitchen, next to the beautiful refectory with its old beams and little decorative touches so typical of this family estate.

Entrance to the cuverie with some of M. Janoueix's antiques

*One of the Great Growths
from St Emilion*

The emphasis here is on family values and respect for tradition. The attention to detail is astonishing, both in the running of the estate and the way the harvesters are looked after. Three generations of the Janoueix family are actively involved in running the estate - they own several other fine properties and a merchant business in Libourne. Before the harvest every picker, about 130 in all, receives a charming letter welcoming them and telling them what is expected of them and what they can expect in return. Many of the pickers are sons and daughters of customers.

Everyone receives a certificate and two bottles of the estate's wine to take home; there are prizes awarded for the best male and female pickers and special awards to long-serving harvesters, presented during a terrific party on the last night.

Lunch is on the tables and the pickers are coming in. Mme Janouiex, carrying a plastic bag full of medicines and other remedies, is searching out the ones who need nursing over a cold or a gastric problem. Vegetable soup is warming after a rather cold morning in the vines. Some people practise the old peasant habit of adding a large glass of wine to the last of their soup (known as *faire Chabrot*). A salad of beetroot and some pâté follows, and then the splendid *entrecôtes à la bordelaise* and big plates of *frites*. All the vegetables and salads are grown on the estate; the poultry and meat used during the harvest are raised here and the pâtés are home-made from the pigs on the farm. The Janouiex's try to serve as many local dishes as possible for their pickers. There is even one dish, *oeufs et braganes en sauce au vin*, made from eggs and little wild leeks that grow between the rows of vines. As the meal is coming to an end, with cheese and *crème renversée*, an impromptu concert starts up - the instruments are only bottles and cutlery, but it is coming from a team of young Danes who have obviously been practising and it sounds good.

Haut Sarpe is unusual in being able to lodge all its pickers in a lovely collection of old farm buildings, a sort of harvest village, with the kitchen and refectory at its centre. There is a benignly paternal atmosphere generated by the family. Leather-bound albums of photographs record past harvests and are regularly added to; a photo-collage of the last year's harvest is on show in the refectory. The family are always pleased when marriages result from harvest encounters, as they often do. Indeed Jean Janouiex met his own wife when she came to pick the harvest as a young woman; now their own children are part of the team.

With a high proportion of young people picking the harvest here, the Janouiex's try hard to make every night a party night. Often there are fancy-dress competitions and this picturesque harvest hamlet's very own disco, the 'Glu-glu-glu', opens after dinner until midnight. 'It's the best night-club in town!' they say and it is probably the only one in the world situated in the middle of vineyards. The music wafts across the courtyard, waking the ducks on the pond and the peacocks in the park of the château; the old buildings look even prettier in the moonlight. It is easy to see how marriages are made at Haut Sarpe.

The 'Glu-glu-glu' night-club in full swing

ENTRECOTE A LA BORDELAISE

A hungry cellar-worker grilling a steak over an improvized fire made from the staves of old barrels steeped in the tannins of Bordeaux wines: these are the supposed origins of this celebrated dish. Who or when are facts that are lost in the usual mists of time. But there are stories of esteemed gastronomes of the past being glad to accept an invitation from a cellar master to share an entrecôte cooked in this way. However, barrels are expensive things nowadays and châteaux are more likely to be selling their old ones than letting their workers use them as cooking fuel. In any case, it gradually became the tradition to use vine-shoots (*sarments*) saved from the pruning, or old vine stocks taken out during re-planting, to make the fire. The ingredients are few and simple but the combination of steak, shallots and marrow has become a classic.

In the absence of old barrels or vine-shoots, the steaks can be grilled over charcoal - not the same, I'm sure the purists would cry, but still pretty good.

According to an often-quoted old book (*'Traîté de Cuisine Bourgeoise Bordelaise'* by Alcide Bontou), the piece of steak should be about the thickness of two fingers. It should be marinaded in a tablespoon of oil, salt and freshly-ground black pepper. When the fire is glowing, put the meat on the grill. Chop together 4 shallots, a good firm piece of beef marrow and a little handful of parsley. Turn the steak and spread this mixture over the upper surface. Heat the blade of the knife and use it to press down the mixture a few times, to soften the marrow. That is all. Any other complications, such as red wine sauces, which sometimes go under the name of *entrecôtes à la bordelaise*, are usually denounced as not being the real thing. (Though they may be a perfectly good thing in their own right - the entrecôte is usually fried in a pan and kept warm while chopped shallots are briefly tossed in the same butter. A teaspoon of flour is then added and a sauce made by adding a glass each of red

Mme Chabrerie grilling the entrecôtes at Château Haut Sarpe

wine and water, to which chopped, raw marrow is added and softened in it. This sometimes appears as *entrecôte marchand du vin*.)

It is useful to know how to prepare the marrow. In *'French Provincial Cooking'*, Elizabeth David advises that the marrow bone should be sawn into 7.5 cm (3 in) lengths by the butcher. If possible, soak the pieces in cold water for 12 to 24 hours, changing the water several times. She explains that this process makes the marrow a better colour, a pale creamy pink, whereas if cooked straight away it tends to be a rather unappetizing grey. Put the bones in cold water to cover, bring slowly to the boil and allow to barely simmer for about 20 minutes. Scoop the marrow out of the bone with the handle of a small spoon. Marrow bones vary in size. Ask the butcher for advice on quantities. It is now ready to chop with the shallots and parsley.

If no marrow bones are obtainable, all is not lost. In the Bordeaux area you see people grilling steaks and simply sprinkling them with a good handful of chopped shallots and parsley. Again, not the same, but good.

IN THE LAND OF THE
REALLY GRAND CHATEAUX

The Médoc takes its name from the Latin *in medio aquae* - it lies between the Atlantic Ocean and the Gironde Estuary. It is flat and the soil is poor - it is a curious fact that vines thrive on the poorest soil, and you see little other vegetation apart from the characteristic pines along the Atlantic coast. If you are in the Médoc you are bound to be on either business or pleasure connected with wine; nothing else seems to happens here and it is on the way to nowhere, unless you count crossing the estuary by ferry.

For many people Margaux, St Julien and the other villages of the Haut-Médoc, with their imposing châteaux and extensive vineyards, epitomize great Bordeaux wines. A large number are owned by absentee landlords - American, Japanese and English multi-national corporations put in managers to run these valuable investments. There is no doubt that this creates a different atmosphere from that of the smaller, family-owned properties around Libourne.

As you drive through the immaculately tended vines, with a rose-bush at the end of each row, there is a plethora of signs with famous names. It seems as if some kind of achitectural competition has taken place here, so varied are the styles. They range from the beautiful eighteenth century Château Beychevelle, to the ultra grand

Château Loudenne in the Médoc is owned by IDV

Château Ducru Beaucaillou, to the Chinese pagoda-like folly which is Cos d'Estournel. Some of them welcome visitors, with regular tours of the *chais*, tastings and even museums. At others entry is strictly by invitation, and those invitations are hard to obtain. Completely and elegantly

restored by its owners, International Distillers and Vintners, Château Loudenne is used for corporate entertaining on a grand scale. In 1980 they re-opened the *cuisine des vendanges* (harvest kitchen) which had previously fallen into disuse. It is now a beautiful L-shaped dining-room with two large fireplaces. Gleaming, copper-covered basins (*chaudrières*) with decorative taps shaped like the head and neck of a goose are set in a blue-and-white tiled *potager* (the same word as is used for a kitchen garden but here it means a kind of

A leading property of the central Médoc

simmering-stove. There are other nice examples at Château Figeac and Château Grand Mayne in St Emilion). This is an outstanding example of an old method of cooking; under the copper basins are holes for the hot coals. It is still used for dishes that need long, slow simmering, such as *jambon au foin* (ham cooked with hay) or *pot-au-feu. Potagers* were also used for keeping soup and vegetables warm. The room is used during the harvest, as well as for dinners throughout the year.

Josette, cook here for 27 years, makes use of the produce grown in the garden. Homemade redcurrant jelly and blackcurrant jam for the visiting customers' breakfasts are in her store-cupboard. She makes an unusual jam from figs, apples and grapes; an old fig tree grows at the entrance to the kitchen and another door gives onto the estate's vines. There are jars of *compote de pommes* for desserts; peaches are made into sorbets. Duck preserved in its own fat (*confit de canard*) and preserved duck livers (*foies gras de canard*) are more of her specialities and *pintade aux figues* and *pintade aux raisins* (guinea-fowl with figs or grapes, see page 84) are favourite ways of using the abundant figs and grapes at harvest time.

Chateau Loudenne's magnificent, restored cuisine des vendanges ➤

TAKE AWAY LUNCH AT LYNCH-BAGES

In the kitchen at Château Lynch-Bages the cooks are cutting up 58 stuffed rabbits which have just come out of the oven ready for the pickers' lunch. A still-life of baskets has been arranged on a big counter under a small window. On closer inspection the baskets are all named. There are one or two old-fashioned looking, metal food containers. There is a sudden whirlwind of activity as the cooks fill the baskets with an assortment of plastic boxes - this is a three-course packed lunch. The window is opened and the pickers come to collect their baskets in relays and take them home to eat. These are locals, many work for the château all through the year and the lady handing out the baskets knows exactly which one belongs to whom, and who likes this and doesn't like that. After lunch the baskets are returned with clean boxes, ready for the evening meal.

Other harvesters - from many different countries and somehow communicating in a variety of languages - are eating the same menu in the refectory. The excellent rabbit is stuffed with pork, onion, garlic, parsley and eggs (see page 83) and is served with a smooth potato purée.

With 85 hectares producing around 35,000 cases, Lynch-Bages is a typical size for the properties here. But it is family-owned, by the Cazes, and run by the dynamic Jean-Michel Cazes, whose style is very different from most Médocains. Having had a successful career in business, he puts the same energy into the family property, as well as managing Château Pichon-Longueville-Baron and Château Cantenac-Brown for the giant French insurance group, Axa.

Lynch-Bages receives literally hundreds of visitors, journalists and camera-crews from all over the world each year; the huge PR operation is headed by Jean-Michel's sister Sylvie, and, like the rest of the business, runs with well-oiled efficiency combined with cosmopolitan friendliness.

Pickers at Château Lynch-Bages collecting their lunch baskets

LE LAPIN FARCI

STUFFED RABBIT FROM CHATEAU LYNCH-BAGES

This is a harvest favourite at Château Lynch-Bages.

FOR 6 PEOPLE
1 large rabbit
butter

FOR THE STUFFING:
20 ml (2 dessertspoons) milk
125 g (4 oz) bread, crusts removed
1 onion
2 cloves garlic
a good handful of fresh parsley
300 g (10 oz) sausagemeat, preferably pure
pork with no rusk or other 'stretchers'
2 eggs
salt and pepper

Preheat the oven to gas mark 6, 400°F, 200°C.

To make the stuffing, warm the milk and soak the bread in it for 10 minutes. Meanwhile, peel and chop the onion and garlic finely. Chop the parsley. Mix with the sausagemeat in a large bowl. Add the milk and bread to this mixture, then incorporate the eggs, one at a time. Season.

Stuff the rabbit with this mixture. Sew up the opening.

Smear the rabbit with butter and roast in the preheated oven for approximately one hour. Baste once or twice during the cooking. If it looks as if it is getting dry, pour a little hot water into the bottom of the roasting pan. You may need to lower the heat half-way through.

Cut up the rabbit and serve, making sure everyone gets some of the stuffing.

LE SALE DE PORC

SALTED PORK WITH VEGETABLES

An old-fashioned peasant dish that the French sigh over nostalgically, this uses an economic cut of pork, which is usually salted nowadays by the charcutier, but used to be salted at home.

Pork takes salting and/or smoking very well. The joint known as petit salé in France is a piece of breast or belly of pork. For this dish, you need to buy a mild-cure, unsmoked bacon joint. Incidentally, the French call bacon 'lard de poitrine' or just 'lard'. A rasher of bacon is 'une tranche de lard', not very often eaten fried or grilled as we do, although during the harvest in the Bordeaux region it is sometimes grilled over vine-shoots. What is known as 'bacon' does not correspond to our bacon at all. What we call lard, they call 'saindoux'. All this can cause confusion when shopping in France.

FOR 6 - 8 PEOPLE
1 kg (2 lb) of mild-cure green bacon in a piece
1 kg (2 lb) carrots
1 kg (2 lb) potatoes
2 medium turnips
1 stick of celery
1 cabbage, usually Savoy but other kinds will do
3 leeks
1 medium onion
2 cloves garlic
salt and pepper
French mustard, to serve

Cover the bacon joint with cold water in a big pot. Bring it to the boil. Skim if necessary. Simmer for 30 minutes.

Meanwhile, prepare the vegetables - peel the carrots, potatoes and turnips, wash the celery, trim the outside leaves from the cabbage and leeks and wash. Peel and coarsely chop the onion and garlic. Cut the cabbage into four, cut any very large potatoes in two. Add all the vegetables to the pot after the first half hour. Season with pepper - as the bacon has been salted you will be unlikely to need salt, check at the end. Bring back just to the boil and simmer very slowly for a further 2 ½ hours. Drain the meat and vegetables (taste the stock - if it is not too salty, it can be used for soup).

Skin the pork, slice and serve on a bed of the vegetables, with a pot of Dijon mustard on the table.

PINTADE AUX FIGUES
ROAST GUINEA-FOWL WITH FIGS

At Château Loudennes, this dish is made using the figs from the old tree which almost blocks the door into the 'cuisine des vendanges'.

FOR 3 - 4 PEOPLE
1 guinea-fowl including giblets (feeds 3, or possibly 4, depending on appetite and what other dishes are served)
butter
6 - 8 figs
beurre manié (a teaspoon of flour with a teaspoon of butter worked into it)
150 ml (5 fl oz) crème fraîche or small glass of Madeira

FOR THE STOCK:
giblets
1 glass white wine
300 ml (½ pint) water
1 onion
1 large carrot
1 stick of celery
1 leek
bouquet garni of parsley, thyme and bay leaf

Preheat the oven to gas mark 6, 400°F, 200°C.

Smear the outside of the guinea-fowl with butter and put a lump inside. Place upside down in a roasting tin and roast in the preheated oven for 20 minutes. Turn breast side up, baste with the juices and continue roasting for another 25 minutes.

Meanwhile, make the stock. Cut up all the vegetables and put them in a pan with the rest of the stock ingredients. Bring to the boil and simmer for about half an hour. Strain and taste. It may need to be reduced by fast boiling for about 5 minutes, to concentrate the flavour.

When the guinea-fowl is cooked, remove from the oven and keep warm while finishing the sauce. Put the figs into the hot oven to warm through. Pour off any fat from the roasting tin, place the tin over a medium heat on top of the cooker and pour in some of the stock. Scrape the bottom of the tin with a wooden spoon to deglaze. Take the tin off the heat and carefully whisk the *beurre manié* into the stock and roasting juices to thicken slightly. When it is incorporated, you can decide whether to add *crème fraîche* or Madeira - either is good. Keep tasting and decide what seasoning is needed. If you feel the sauce is too thick, add more stock.

Keep the sauce warm while you carve the guinea-fowl. Quarter the figs and arrange with the meat on a serving dish. Pour over the sauce and serve.

PINTADE AUX RAISINS
GUINEA-FOWL WITH GRAPES

Josette, the cook at Château Loudennes, can open the back door and step into the vineyards to pick a handful of grapes for this dish. Cabernet or Merlot grapes are very unlikely to be available in the supermarket, so we must improvize. Large and very sweet grapes would not be suitable. If possible choose small, dark-skinned grapes. Wine grapes tend to have thick skins and not as much juice as table grapes. If you are eating this dish surrounded by great vineyards, drinking with it the wine of the château, the fact that you have to spit out a lot of pips probably does not bother you. In other circumstances, seedless grapes might be an improvement.

The method is the same as for guinea-fowl with figs, but at the end, the grapes are warmed in the sauce before it is poured over the bird. Sometimes it is served with both figs and grapes.

BLANQUETTE DE VEAU
VEAL STEW WITH ONIONS AND MUSHROOMS

The veal is cooked in stock with vegetables to make the basis of this comforting dish. The stock is then used to make a sauce, which is finished with cream and egg yolks. It is certainly not a difficult dish but there are several distinct steps and it will take about 2 ¼ hours to prepare and cook. It's a good example of the French repertoire of family dishes, coming a day or two after a chicken dish which will have produced a stock, and is not extravagant because it uses cheap cuts of meat, cooked slowly and with care. Only a small amount of cream is needed but, with the egg yolks, it is enough to make the sauce seem luxurious.

It only takes a little practice to move from one step to another smoothly and it gets easier each time it is made. It can be prepared ahead of time up to the point when the veal and onions are united with the sauce and mushrooms. One or two corners can be cut: it can be made without stock (better to use water than a stock cube) simply by increasing the number of vegetables and adding a glass of wine. Leave the vegetables with the veal in the final dish if you like. The mushrooms can be omitted: the dish is not so fine - but still good. It can also be made using lamb.

FOR 6 - 8 PEOPLE
1.5 kg (3 lb) boned stewing veal - a mixture of breast, short ribs from best end, shoulder, middle neck, scrag and knuckle. Very often the butcher will just offer 'stewing veal' which will probably be a mixture of these cuts. It is useful to have some gelatinous meat in the mixture.
1 onion
1 large carrot
2 celery stalks
bouquet garni of parsley, thyme and bay leaf
salt and whole black peppercorns
1 - 1.5 litres (2 - 2 ½ pints) chicken stock

TO FINISH:
about 20 very small onions (often sold for pickling) or 6 small onions
3 tablespoons butter
2 tablespoons flour
250 g (8 oz) small mushrooms, wiped clean

lemon juice
salt and pepper
150 ml (¼ pint) double or whipping cream
3 egg yolks

First cut the veal into cubes. Put them into a pan, cover amply with cold water and bring to the boil. Simmer for a few minutes - grey scum will rise to the surface. Drain into a colander and run under the cold tap to get rid of the scum. It may seem tempting to eliminate this small step, but it is important for the final flavour and appearance.

Now the veal is to be cooked with the stock and vegetables. Put the meat into a casserole with the onion, carrot, celery, *bouquet garni*, a pinch of salt, 6 black peppercorns and the stock, which should just cover the meat. Bring just to the boil, cover and simmer very slowly for about 1½ hours. Test after 1 ¼ hours by sticking a fork into the meat - it should feel tender without falling apart.

If you have been able to buy little onions, they must be peeled and cooked whole in some of the stock. Otherwise, peel and cut the onions in four. Take a ladleful out of the casserole and simmer them in a small pan for about 30 minutes.

Once the veal is cooked, drain it, keeping the stock ready to make the sauce. Rinse the casserole.

Melt the butter in a pan and stir in the flour. When smoothly amalgamated, start adding the stock. You may not need all of it. The sauce should not be very thick and there should be enough to cover the veal when you return it to the pan. Simmer for a few minutes - if a skin forms on top, skim it off. Add the mushrooms and simmer for 10 minutes. Taste the sauce after this and add salt, pepper and lemon juice, as necessary. The lemon juice is important to balance the cream and egg yolks, so at this stage the sauce should taste quite lemony.

Put the veal and the onions into the casserole, pour the sauce over them and bring back to simmering point. Meanwhile, whisk the egg yolks and cream together in a bowl. Take a ladleful of the sauce and beat into the egg and cream mixture. Pour it all into the casserole and mix with the rest of the sauce. It should only cook for a few more minutes and should not boil. The *blanquette* is usually served with boiled rice, noodles or steamed potatoes.

POULE AU BOUILLON FARCIE OR POULE AU POT
STUFFED BOILED CHICKEN

There are many versions of this dish which must have originated as a way to make a tough old bird tender. By stuffing it and simmering for a long time with many vegetables, it became a more interesting dish and fed more people. The stuffing usually incorporates the chicken liver, bread soaked in milk and some meat either in the form of ham or minced veal or pork.

FOR 6 PEOPLE
1 boiling fowl including giblets, total weight about 2 kg (4 lb)

FOR THE STUFFING:
200 g (7 oz) white bread, crusts removed
a little milk
200 g (7 oz) minced veal or pork
1 thick slice of raw ham (jambon cru, or jambon de Bayonne - if these are not available Parma ham is suitable)
2 tablespoons chopped onion
approximately 1 tablespoon butter
2 cloves garlic, chopped
the chicken liver, and the gizzard, if liked
1 tablespoon of chopped fresh parsley
1 teaspoon of dried thyme
salt and pepper
grated nutmeg
2 eggs

VEGETABLES FOR THE POT:
2 medium onions
4 medium carrots
2 turnips
2 sticks of celery
2 leeks
bouquet garni of parsley, thyme and bay leaf

To make the stuffing, soak the bread in milk for a few minutes, then squeeze fairly dry and put in a bowl large enough for all the rest of the stuffing ingredients. Add the minced meat. Chop the raw ham and add.

Cook the onion in the butter slowly until soft, then add to the bowl with the garlic. Clean the chicken liver and chop it with the gizzard if used, and add. Add the herbs and seasoning. Finally add the two eggs and stir it all until well mixed.

Stuff the chicken with this mixture and sew up the opening so that the stuffing does not escape during the cooking. (Special large needles and fine string are sold for this purpose in kitchen equipment shops.)

Put the chicken in a large flameproof pot with all the vegetables, peeled and roughly chopped, and the *bouquet garni*. Cover with water and bring to the boil. Any scum rising to the top should be skimmed off. Turn the heat down as low as possible, cover and simmer for about 3 hours - it is hard to be precise about a boiling fowl - you want the meat to be tender, just beginning to come off the bone easily, but not overcooked so that it becomes stringy. To serve, cut up the chicken and surround with the vegetables and stuffing.

VARIATIONS ON CLASSIC DISHES
❖ *As these vegetables have given all their goodness to the stock (which will make an excellent soup), some people remove the vegetables from the stock about 30 minutes before they judge the chicken to be ready and replace them with a fresh selection, including potatoes if liked. It certainly makes a finer dish. Little pickled gherkins can also be served with it.*

❖ *Sometimes the chicken is served with rice that has been cooked in some of the stock.*

❖ *'Poule farcie à la bordelaise' is made with a more sophisticated stuffing, including truffles and mushrooms, although the method is more or less the same. The truth is, there are many versions, which claim to be 'à la bordelaise'.*

❖ *'Poule au pot-au-feu' is a variation of the recipe on page 32, using a boiling fowl instead of beef.*

❖ *If you can get boiling fowl, all these recipes are worth trying. People often complain that chickens are tasteless nowadays, but boiling fowl usually have lots of flavour.*

POULE AU RIZ A LA CREME
CHICKEN WITH RICE AND A CREAM SAUCE

This comforting dish has much in common with a blanquette. Like the preceding dish, it is simmered slowly in stock with vegetables; some of the stock is used to make a sauce, to which you add cream and egg yolks and some to cook the rice to serve with it. Boiling fowl are not always available although it is sometimes possible to order one from a good butcher.

FOR 6 PEOPLE
100 g (4 oz) unsmoked streaky bacon
*1 boiling fowl including giblets, total weight
about 2 kg (4 lb)*
2 onions, sliced
4 carrots, sliced
*2.25 litres (4 pints) stock, either made
from the giblets and some veal bones, or saved from
another boiled chicken dish*
bouquet garni of parsley, thyme and bay leaf
2 cloves garlic
375 g (12 oz) white long-grain rice
45 g (1½ oz) butter
2 tablespoons plain flour
2 egg yolks
250 ml (8 fl oz) single cream
lemon juice

Lay the slices of bacon on the bottom of a heavy flameproof casserole - oval is best for a chicken. Put in the chicken and surround with the onions and carrots. Cook over a moderate heat until the bacon fat melts - do not let it get so hot that it burns. Meanwhile, heat the stock in another pan. When the bacon is ready, add the hot stock, *bouquet garni* and garlic, cover and simmer gently for 2½ to 3 hours.

About 30 minutes before the chicken is ready, measure out 1 litre (1¾ pints) of stock from the casserole. Put 750 ml (1¼ pints) into a pan with the rice and 15 g (½ oz) of the butter and bring to the boil. Turn down the heat. Cover with foil and a tight-fitting lid and cook on the lowest possible heat for about 25 minutes without lifting the lid. Turn off the heat and leave another 5 minutes before taking the lid off and turning out onto a dish.

Once the rice is simmering, start making the sauce. Melt the rest of the butter in a pan, stir in the flour and cook for 2 to 3 minutes, then gradually add the remaining 300 ml (½ pint) of warm stock. Stir over the heat for a few minutes as it thickens. Make sure it is smooth. Beat the egg yolks in a small bowl with a tablespoon of the cream. Add the rest of the cream to the sauce and let it simmer for about 5 minutes. Take a spoonful of the hot sauce and stir it into the egg mixture, then mix this into the sauce. Stir it for a few more minutes over the gentle heat, then taste for seasoning. It needs a squeeze of lemon to give it some acidity or it will be too blandly creamy.

Remove the chicken from the pot. Pour the remaining stock through a sieve and reserve, discarding the bacon and vegetables. This stock is useful for making soup.

Carve the chicken and arrange on a dish with the sauce poured over. Serve the rice separately. *Poule au riz* is usually served without vegetables but is nice followed by a green salad with quite a sharp vinaigrette.

PETIT SALE AUX LENTILLES
SALTED PORK WITH LENTILS

The bacon joint is boiled and served on a bed of lentils, which is an excellent combination. The best kind of lentils to use are small, round and dark, known as Puy; the green-brown, flatter kind are fine; orange ones are not, as they cook to a mush.

FOR 6 - 8 PEOPLE
1 k g (2 lb) mild-cure green bacon in one piece
2 - 3 shallots, peeled
bouquet garni of parsley, thyme and bay leaf
1 leek, cleaned and chopped
2 carrots, chopped
6 black peppercorns
500 g (1 lb) lentils, preferably Puy

Soak the lentils in cold water overnight.

Cover the bacon joint with cold water in a pan. Bring slowly to the boil, then simmer for 30 minutes. Drain and put the joint in fresh water to cover. Add the vegetables, *bouquet garni* and peppercorns. Bring to the boil and simmer slowly for about an hour.

Meanwhile, drain the lentils and rinse, then boil until soft but not disintegrating - this will probably take about an hour, but some cook more quickly, according to how old they are - it is best to test them after 30 minutes. Drain, stir in a knob of butter, then season with salt and pepper and a squeeze of lemon. Delicious, served with the slices of hot bacon joint arranged on top and Dijon mustard.

HACHIS PARMENTIER

You hear French people sighing over the memory of a good hachis Parmentier in a way English people rarely do over a cottage pie, to which it is closely related. Perhaps this is because we have managed to debase a perfectly good family dish, so that it is now most frequently encountered in a ubiquitous commercial version, microwaved at our convenience in a pub. By contrast, hachis Parmentier is not a thing you see on a menu in France. However, families usually love it and it is a favourite dish for the harvesters. The dish takes its name from Antoine-Auguste Parmentier, an agronomist who, in the late eighteenth century, successfully encouraged the French to regard potatoes as a worthwhile food.

As Mme Goullée pronounced, hachis Parmentier cannot be made from fresh meat - well, of course it could be, but that would defeat the object. It is a dish to make when you have a sufficient quantity of well-flavoured left-over meat for your family. During the harvest it is most frequently made with left-over boiled beef from a pot-au-feu. This can be supplemented with any meat left from a roast, usually beef but it can be a mixture. It is impossible to give exact quantities but here is the method.

Make a smooth and creamy potato purée with plenty of butter and milk. It should not be stiff and certainly not lumpy, and should be well-seasoned.

Mince the meat, then add to a pan in which some chopped onions have been softened in butter. Now add a good handful (or more depending on the amount of meat) of fresh parsley. Other fresh herbs could be used instead if available, otherwise use dried ones. Season well and moisten with some stock from the pot-au-feu or juices kept from the roast. It should not be sloppy, but neither should it be dry.

Take a gratin dish, butter it and spread half the purée over the bottom. Now spread the meat mixture over this. Spread the rest of the purée over the top. Dot with butter. Put it into the oven at about gas mark 4, 350°F, 180°C for approximately half an hour, until the whole is piping hot and the top is appetizingly brown with crunchy bits round the edge.

There are as many 'correct' ways of doing this as there are cooks. In one version, soft, white breadcrumbs are mixed with the meat and milk is used to moisten it; in another, the meat and potato purée are mixed together in the gratin dish. It is up to the cook to improvize.

Petit salé aux lentilles - salted pork with lentils

Figues au vin rouge - figs in red wine

FIGUES AU VIN ROUGE

FIGS IN RED WINE

Wine-makers often have to open several bottles at a time so that customers can taste their range of wines in the different vintages; the remains of the bottles are generally used to top up barrels. Sometimes they find their way into the family's vinegar barrel or into the kitchen, where inspired combinations may evolve. Figs in red wine is one such partnership. Figs are in season at the time of the harvest, so if the grower has a tree in his courtyard, this luxurious dish is often enjoyed by the pickers. It is considered that these figs improve if prepared the day before they are to be eaten.

FOR 6 - 8 PEOPLE

24 ripe figs, wiped clean
500 ml (15 fl oz) red wine
125 g (4 oz) caster sugar
3 or 4 drops vanilla essence
1 pinch of ground allspice or a
mixture of nutmeg, cloves and
cinnamon or ginger

Quarter the figs without cutting right through the skin - just open them up. Arrange them in one layer in a flameproof casserole.

In another pan, bring the wine to the boil with the sugar, vanilla essence and allspice, then pour over the figs. Simmer for 10 minutes. Put aside to cool.

Lift out the figs and arrange in bowls, then pour over some of the wine. Serve chilled.

PECHES AU VIN ROUGE

PEACHES IN RED WINE

In years when the harvest is early enough and peaches abundant, these two recipes, or variations of them, are used in many wine-growing areas.

1ST VERSION FOR 6 PEOPLE

approximately 1 kg (2 lb) ripe peaches
(at least one peach per person)
1 bottle red wine
1 tablespoon kirsch, optional
200 g (7 oz) caster sugar

Pour boiling water over the peaches, leave for 5 minutes, then plunge them into cold water and peel them. Cut them in half and take out the stones. Slice evenly. Marinade the peaches overnight in the wine, kirsch and sugar. That is all. The kirsch is a refinement; it can be made without it or you could experiment with other fruit brandies.

2ND VERSION

This takes the same ingredients but with small peaches, if possible. Peel the peaches as before, but leave them whole. Marinate overnight as for the first version. The next day poach them in the marinade for about ten minutes, then lift them out and drain. Reduce the marinade by fast boiling by about a quarter, until it is just slightly syrupy. Pour over the peaches and cool. This dish is best if made the previous day and kept in the fridge.

COMPOTE DE POMMES

A compote is simply a way of poaching fresh or dried fruit in a light syrup, but most apple compotes are different, nearer to being purées or apple sauces.

This is one way to make an apple compote. Take good eating apples, peel, core and slice them into an enamelled cast-iron casserole, squeezing lemon juice over the slices. Sprinkle them with vanilla-flavoured sugar, cover and simmer over a low heat or in a low temperature oven. If you are worried that they will catch or burn on the bottom of the pan, add 1 tablespoon of water, but this is really unnecessary if they cook slowly enough. They should be ready in about half an hour, depending on the variety used and how much you want the fruit to retain the shape of its slices. The apples are at their best served warm or hot. They can be accompanied by slices of gâteau au vin blanc (see page 117) or with little cakes or biscuits.

Honey can be used instead of sugar, in which case a little cinnamon sprinkled over the slices is good.

PECHES DES VIGNES ET PRUNEAUX D'AGEN AU VIN ROUGE

VINEYARD PEACHES AND DRIED AGEN PLUMS IN WINE

It used to be the custom in some wine-growing areas to plant peach trees in the vineyards. They gave shade for the vineyard workers to rest and eat under, as well as small, well-flavoured fruit. You occasionally still see them in the Côte d'Or in Burgundy, although the land is now so valuable that it has become uneconomic to cultivate anything but vines, which are planted in the uninterrupted lines most practical for getting the tractors in and out. These little peaches are sometimes for sale in French markets as pêches des vignes.

Prunes from Agen are reputed to be the very best - they certainly are delicious and moist. Jane Grigson in her 'Fruit Book' tells us that Agen has a splendid market on Sundays at which you can buy these and many other dried fruits from the area. She also explains that Californian prunes come from the same strain which was originally taken there from Agen. The relevant point is that for this recipe you need small, tasty peaches with white flesh and dusty-looking pink skins and large, juicy prunes. The original recipe used wine from Cahors, made from one of the lesser-known Bordeaux grapes, the Malbec, which was known as 'the black wine of Cahors'. The fashion now is for lighter coloured wines, so a Cabernet Sauvignon, which is not too tannic, from the Bordeaux region or the New World, could be substituted.

FOR 6 - 8 PEOPLE
2 kg (4 lb) small peaches
twice as many prunes as peaches
1 bottle red wine
250 g (8 oz) caster sugar
a stick of cinnamon
12 peppercorns
12 coriander seeds

Pour boiling water over the peaches, leave for 5 minutes, then plunge them into cold water and peel them. (It is not absolutely necessary to do this - some people leave the skins on.) Cut them in half and remove the stones. You should now have an equal quantity of peach halves and prunes.

Put the wine, sugar and spices into an enamelled pan and bring to the boil. Add the peaches and prunes and simmer until the fruit are cooked, about 15 to 20 minutes - longer if they were under-ripe. Put aside to cool, then chill in the fridge overnight. Place a prune in each peach half and arrange the fruit in a bowl. Sieve the wine to remove the spices and pour it over the fruit.

OEUFS AU LAIT
BAKED CUSTARD

These individual baked custards can easily be made in quantity, as long as you have a large oven and enough little Pyrex or other oven-proof ramekins, so they are a frequent harvest dessert. They may be served as an accompaniment to a compote, or on their own with biscuits. The changes may be rung by flavouring them with vanilla, grated lemon peel, chocolate or coffee, or by coating the bottom of the pots with caramel first (put a couple of tablespoons of white sugar into a heavy-bottomed pan over a high heat, until it changes colour to dark brown, then pour quickly into the ramekins before it sets hard) to make a caramel cream or crème renversée. They can be served unmoulded.

FOR 6 PEOPLE

For 6 ramekins (capacity about 125 ml/4 fl oz)
2 medium eggs
300 ml (½ pint) milk
15 g (½ oz) caster sugar
4 drops vanilla essence
butter for greasing

Preheat the oven to gas mark 2, 300°F, 150°C.

Break the eggs into a bowl. Lightly beat them with a fork. Add the milk, sugar and vanilla and stir to mix well.

Butter the ramekins. Strain the mixture through a sieve into a jug. Fill the ramekins with the mixture. Arrange them in a roasting tin; pour in cold water to reach half-way up the ramekins.

Bake in the preheated oven for 20 to 30 minutes. If they cook too long or too fast they will form a tough skin on top and/or curdle. Check after 20 minutes - give a ramekin a little nudge to see if it has set.

VIN CHAUD AUX EPICES
HOT SPICED WINE

This is served at Haut Sarpe to warm up the pickers when they get back from the vines. There are those who advocate various additions, even including tea! But basically this is wine heated with sugar and spices, sieved and drunk as hot as possible.

FOR 6 - 8 PEOPLE

1 bottle of an every-day drinking red wine -
nothing too subtle
about 1 tablespoon lemon juice
1 stick of cinnamon
1 clove
1 vanilla pod
a pinch of grated nutmeg
125 g (4 oz) caster sugar or if liked,
a light brown sugar

Simply place all the ingredients in a pan, bring slowly to the boil, then serve straightaway.

VARIATIONS ON CLASSIC DISHES

❖ *Some people suggest infusing the wine and spices for some time before heating, so as to get a spicier flavour. Many people add a dash of fruit brandy, cognac, marc (distilled from the skins and pips after the grape harvest) or a liqueur just before serving.*

❖ *In the Loire, the local vin doux is used instead of red wine, in which case the amount of sugar is reduced.*

L O I R E

The valley of the great river Loire is well known for its soft beautiful light, beloved by painters, and for its many great châteaux and fine gardens, as well as for its vineyards. What must strike anyone in search of those vineyards is the great distance you must drive if you wish to visit them all. But it is a journey well worth making, with beautiful changing scenery as you cross and re-cross the meandering river and its many tributaries and with opportunities to visit the markets of the region.

◄ *The Domaine aux Moines, Savennières*

The flower market held every Saturday on the Boulevard du Maréchal Foch in Angers is particularly notable. In terms of wine, the area just south-east of the mouth of the Loire is known as Muscadet. Nearby Nantes is the town which has given its name to the sauce *beurre Nantais*, also known as *beurre blanc* (see page 108), which often accompanies the *alose* (the seawater shad which spawns in rivers), *sandre* (the freshwater pike-perch), or *brochet* (pike) fished in the river Loire. The Muscadet is a large vineyard area, producing mainly white wine which is from one grape type, now called the Muscadet grape but originating in Burgundy where it was known as the Melon de Bourgogne. This produces the crisp white wine which is so often served in France with seafood, particularly oysters, mussels and crabs. That of Sèvre et Maine has the highest reputation and the best wines are bottled straight from the vat, *sur lies* (unfiltered), and have a refreshing little tingle on the tongue.

Moving eastwards up-river, we come to the town of Angers (which also lays claim to the *beurre blanc* - and it is true that the shallots which are a vital ingredient are grown around here). Red, rosé and white wines, both dry and sweet, are all made in the Anjou. The white grape here is the Chenin Blanc, which in Savennières produces an unusual dry white as well as a sweet wine.

South of the river - so many times do you find yourself crossing a bridge here it is sometimes hard to remember which bank of the river you are on - the best dessert wines of the Loire are produced in Quarts de Chaume, Côteaux du Layon and Bonnezeaux. It is the local habit to drink these rich, sweet wines with the great pork dishes and, in particular, the wide range of *charcuterie* for which the region is renowned.

Towards Tours one finds the red wine Saumur Champigny, which is deliciously fruity when drunk young. It is made from the Cabernet Franc which is also the grape widely planted in Bordeaux around St Emilion. Chinon and Bourgueil are the two Loire red wines most often considered for ageing; production is tiny, which accounts for the fact that they were relatively unknown until recently.

Along this stretch of the river are some of the great châteaux and early churches for which the Loire is famed. In a number of villages the houses seem to have been grafted onto cliffs. Numerous caves in these cliffs provide perfect natural conditions for the cultivation of mushrooms; there is even a little museum of mushroom culture near Saumur.

From Saumur up to Vouvray, sparkling white wine is made using the champagne method (*méthode champenoise*) and sold as Crémant de Loire. Dry, medium-dry and sweet white wines of the area are also made. These sweeter wines (on the label they may be described as *doux*), while not finding an appreciative market very often in the U.K. or U.S.A., nevertheless seem in keeping with the lush scenery of the Loire river and go well with some of the local dishes. Although it may seem strange to marry a sweet wine with fish, it can balance the acidity of the *beurre blanc* which is the usual accompaniment to the whole poached fish served in the restaurants along the banks of the river. A more obvious combination is made between these wines and the wonderful fruit of the area used in open tarts.

For many, the most important wine-growing area of the Loire valley is Sancerre and its neighbour, Pouilly Fumé. Here the Sauvignon Blanc grape is planted on gently sloping hillsides (although some can be vertiginous, like the Monts Damnés in Chavignol), producing a white wine combining qualities of pungent fruitiness with acidity, which makes it ideal as an appetite-awakening aperitif. Alongside the vineyards are the goat farms which produce the celebrated crottins de Chavignol - delicious little cheeses which can be eaten fresh or slightly aged. The wines have become quite high-priced, but not far away are the villages of Ménétou-Salon, Quincy and Reuilly where the Sauvignon Blanc grape gives wines which are cheaper and well worth exploring.

Although vines have become important to the economy of the Loire, it was not always so. This was, and to quite a large extent still is, an area of mixed farming. In the Muscadet, where real poverty was experienced by smallholders until well after the last war, the production of linen was as important, if not more so, than wine.

That mixed farming continues is one of the pleasures of travelling in the Loire. One may round a corner in the high plâteau of the Anjou to find a brightly-coloured strip of flowers being harvested for market. One passes through vineyards, then maize, asparagus, or arable land. Here *fermes-auberges* (farms serving meals and sometimes providing simple accommodation) still exist, serving excellent local food in basic but friendly surroundings. These establishments are often booked by wine-growers for their end of harvest celebrations.

Picknicking on *rillettes* (local pâté, see page 105), goat cheeses and local wine, sitting in a clover field with corn-flowers and poppies all around, looking across at the old walled town of Sancerre on its hilltop, vines in the middle distance, goats grazing in the foreground, you feel that the drive of more than 400 kilometres from the mouth of the Loire, is, as the Michelin Guide might say, well worth the detour.

Poor weather conditions for the pickers in Sancerre

LINEN AND MUSCADET -
PRE-WAR LIFE IN THE VINES

Listening to the rumbustious, splendidly mousta-chioed Jean-Yves Secher discussing the harvest dishes of his childhood with his wife and mother is like being buffeted by a strong but warm wind. There are fierce arguments about details - amicably resolved - and strongly held views about social change, and much laughter too.

This family, who make Muscadet de Sèvre et Maine Clos des Bourguignons (so-called because it was one of the original vineyards planted with Melon de Bourgogne vines in the eighteenth century), used to lodge and feed forty pickers, but since 1984 they have used a picking machine. For Jean-Yves it was the new laws raising the basic agricultural wage, introduced in 1968, which proved a turning point. Until then little had changed in this rural community.

The picture of the past that emerged was of a hard life, with few luxuries or entertainments. Here vines and flax, liking the same kind of soil, were both cultivated. Most *vignerons* kept a pig, one or two cows and some hens. There were few shops, just the grocer for essentials; little was eaten that was not grown or raised on the farm.

Sur lie Muscadet from an historic vineyard

Mme Secher senior remembered harvest food before the war: *café-au-lait*, bread and butter first thing, then a mid-day meal, which was carried up to the vines in baskets on the back and consisted of a dish of beans, or a salad, a home-reared chicken, duck or rabbit and possibly a piece of Camembert, although cheese was generally considered to be a luxury at that time. In the evening there would be a bowl of soup - probably *soupe aux choux* (cabbage soup, see page 132), or *soupe au pain* (bread soup, see below) followed by fruit, *pêches des vignes*, the little peaches from

A distant view of the Loire from the vineyards

the trees often planted in the vineyards, or apples or pears from the orchard.

This is their recipe for *la pannade* - bread soup (also known locally as *la mittonée*):

Water, bread, butter, salt, sometimes milk, are the ingredients of this homely soup. The bread and water are gently simmered until the bread is broken down ('until it is like glue,' said one member of the Secher family), then a lump of butter, salt and a little milk is added. This is a thick concoction - Jean-Yves said 'the spoon stands up in it,' but this was hotly disputed by other members of the family. The kind of bread used came from the big loaves of country bread which could weigh three kilos (six pounds) - they were made with unrefined flour and had a lot more goodness and fibre in them than most modern French bread. The soup was also eaten in the mornings at breakfast by Mme Secher's grandparents before they went into the vines.

Les trempinettes (although sweet, this was eaten as a first course - it seems closely related to the kind of possets and caudles popular in eighteenth-century Britain) as told by the Secher family:

'You put sugar in a tureen and pour in some hot water. Then you add toast, cut up small, and then some wine, red or white as you please and stir gently. You put in as much sugar as is to your taste, and as many litres of wine as you like - and a glass of *eau de vie* if you like. If you like a lot of sugar then you need lots of wine! You eat it with a spoon, like a soup. It must be freshly made.'

Here in the Loire, the pig supplies the ingredients for many of the best dishes and it was usual to kill one before the harvest. Hams were cured; sausages made, some to be smoked in the chimney; bacon joints were salted in *charniers* (large earthenware salting pots), later to be soaked in fresh water, boiled with herbs for 1 ½ hours and eaten cold in slices; *rillons* (see page 105) - *richauds*, *rillauds* and *rillots* are all alternative names for the same dish which is rather confusing! - made from the unsalted belly of pork; *rillettes* made similarly but without the extra chunks of pork (see page 105); and *boulettes* (see page 110) - another economical dish - were made, sometimes with pork or with a mixture of pork and rabbit.

The Sechers described two old-fashioned harvest pork dishes of which they used to be fond, but which are rarely seen now:

La Pire (local patois word, a kind of *civet* of liver)
This is made using pork liver cooked in wine and a little water, with lots of onions, parsley, thyme, and little bits of streaky bacon, for half a day. The mixture was chopped coarsely after cooking and put into earthenware terrines. It was eaten cold with bread.

La Fressure (a kind of brawn)
A pig's head is boiled in water in a large *marmite* or stock-pot, with onions, rind from the other joints, parsley and thyme. When cooked, the bones are removed and the meat is minced. The stock is kept and reheated. Over a gentle heat the pig's blood is added, then seasoned with salt, pepper and cinnamon. Now it must be stirred continuously and watched so it does not boil - blood is 'very delicate' - until it thickens. This can be kept for several days, then slices can be cut and warmed before serving.

At the Domaine aux Moines in Savennières a different, calmer atmosphere prevails. A small country road winds out of the quiet little town of Savennières (where there is an excellent *charcuterie artisanale*, making many of the local pork specialities) up into the steeper vineyards. The Loire can be glimpsed in the distance. At the time of the harvest, the glowing, autumnal reds of the Virginia creeper which covers the old vat-house and farm buildings make a beautiful sight. Tiny pink cyclamen are in flower at the foot of the walls and under trees which surround this lovely house. A terrace running the length of the house gives onto a formal garden which, in 1930, was restored and laid out as it was when monks cultivated the vines here in the Middle Ages.

An efficient manager, Mme Laroche combines the use of modern aids, such as a freezer, with a respect for old standards. Hens are kept, a kitchen garden provides vegetables and fruit, a pig is reared and killed in good time for the harvest.

As much as possible is done ahead of time, because during the harvest Mme Laroche is busy in the vines supervising the picking, to-ing and fro-ing in an old truck between vines, vat-house and kitchen, with not much time to cook.

A red wine from Cabernet Franc

Joints of pork to roast are prepared and frozen, ready to be cooked and served to her small team of about ten pickers - her grown-up children are joined by other students and her two permanent cellar-workers and there are one or two local people who go home for lunch; *rillettes* and terrines are made and, in the traditional way, nothing of the pig is wasted.

The domaine mainly makes dry white wine from its nine hectares, although one small parcel of vines across the road from the house is planted with the Cabernet grape to make an excellent and rare red Savennières. Despite being a small estate, the harvest takes three weeks, for they pass twice or sometimes three times through the same vineyards, selecting and picking the grapes as they reach ripeness.

The pickers here make their own breakfast, boiling

any number of eggs fresh from the hens to have with their bread or brioches.

Favourite dishes include those roasts of pork, the first week cooked slowly with onions, tomatoes and potatoes (see page 110) and, to ring the changes later in the *vendanges*, spread with mustard, wrapped in *pâtes feuilletés* and accompanied by whole garlic cloves baked in their skins (see page 111) and plenty of *frites*.

Boudins noirs (black puddings) are made - these darkly gleaming coils are perhaps an acquired taste, but there are those for whom they are a great gastronomic treat despite their humble, not to say frugal, origins. A local version, known as *la gogue* is unusual in that it contains many green vegetables - chard, lettuces and leeks amongst them - and is very large. At the Domaine aux Moines the *boudins* are served in the traditional French way, sliced and grilled, accompanied by sweet apples, sliced and tossed in butter, and a smooth, creamy purée of potatoes.

Chickens are either roasted plainly, or cut up and sautéed in butter with mustard, lemon juice and curry powder and served with rice. *Poulet Angevine*, a local dish, is also served (see page 114).

Mme Laroche always roasts a turkey at least once during the harvest, serving the white meat at lunch and using the carcass with the brown meat to make a good stock to be served with lots of vegetables cooked in it, for the evening meal.

For *lapin à la moutarde* (see page 115), a rabbit cut in pieces is sautéed, then coated with mustard; a little cognac is poured over and flamed, and the dish is simmered in the oven. Just before serving a pot of *crème fraîche* is added to the cooking juices to make a sauce.

The Laroches have an orchard full of fruit trees and most of their desserts make good use of this. They always have a glut of pears at the time of the harvest and hardly a day goes by without at least one pear tart being eaten (see page 119).

Lapin à la moutarde - rabbit in a mustard and cream sauce

ONION SOUP FOR BREAKFAST
IN THE ANJOU

Vignerons in Anjou and Touraine more often than not find themselves harvesting late in October - and October in the vines can be cold. Further south, with earlier harvests, pickers are usually dressed in T-shirts, and in some hot years bikinis and bare torsos are *de rigueur* amongst the rows. But here oilskins and heavy jerseys are more suitable as early morning temperatures come close to freezing. A good breakfast is called for, thinks the Biotteau family.

Their large, well-placed house commands a beautiful view over the surrounding countryside. It has substantial farm buildings, vat-house and kitchen garden. Their own produce - pigs, hens, ducks, guinea-fowl, rabbits, vegetables and fruit - is used for the harvest meals. A well-equipped modern refectory and kitchens have been built to serve the hundred or so pickers in the autumn and are available for hire throughout the year for weddings or other receptions.

The copious breakfast served to put their harvesters in good heart on a cold, raw morning very often starts with an onion soup (see page 104). Homemade *rillettes* also keep the cold out, and so do *côtes de porc*, a piece of pork loin, roasted in the oven, and eaten cold with mustard. There is plenty of fresh bread and homemade butter to go with the *charcuterie*. *Tartines des graisses* are popular; these are slices of the fattier belly of pork joint, roasted and when cold, sliced, spread with mustard and eaten on bread. If the morning is really chilly, hot sugared wine is sent up to the vineyards.

Drawing on the farm's resources, the Domaine Biotteau serve plenty of vegetable soups, and salads of beetroot, grated raw carrot and tomatoes make an *hors d'oeuvre* with homemade pâtés. There are four ladies at work in the kitchen, including the Biotteau's daughters and daughters-in- law, making pâtés and terrines and preparing the farm's poultry and other produce. Catherine Biotteau, who has married into another local wine-making family, the Richous, fondly recalls her childhood memories of the communal life lived at the time of the harvest and the feeling of working together.

At mid-day there is always a meat dish - beefsteak with *frites*, pork chops with sauté potatoes, beef simmered in wine, various *ragoûts* (see page 114 for *ragoût de canard*) or *coq au vin* (see page 40) using their own poultry. *Boudins noirs* are sliced and grilled as described opposite, but here they are often accompanied by a dish of semi-dried haricot beans - called *les grenots* locally. These need to be shelled, then simmered in water with an onion and *bouquet garni* for about an hour until tender and served with 'a good salad of *endive* with garlic,' according to Mme Biotteau.

In every harvest cook's mind some dishes are for mid-day and others for evening - it seems to be an unwritten rule. In general, evening meals are lighter on the digestion and there is more likely to be a dessert. One of the Biotteau's supper dishes for the pickers is made from pig's liver. It is both simple and economical. The liver is sliced and browned in a little butter in a frying pan, then lifted out so that a sauce can be made in the same pan. This uses lots of finely chopped onions, or shallots if available. Adding more butter if necessary, they are cooked until soft, a little flour is added to the pan and some *vin doux* (local sweet white wine) to make enough sauce to cover the slices of liver which are now put back in the pan, and simmered for 30 minutes. This is 'liver and onions' the French way.

Desserts in the evening often consist of a compote of apples or other fruit with a *gâteau au vin blanc* (see page 117). Sometimes pears baked whole in the oven are served. This is a simple idea for making good use of cooking pears or windfall fruit. It takes no preparation except to put the clean, unpeeled fruit on a baking tray and into a medium oven. They emerge with all their juices intact about an hour later (sooner if smaller).

OLD FRIENDS AND FEASTING CHEZ COTAT IN CHAVIGNOL

The harvest at this small (they only need about a dozen pickers) but distinguished estate in Chavignol, near Sancerre, is always done by volunteers, friends from M. Cotat's army days - a kind of mini regimental reunion. When you meet Mme Cotat it is easy to understand why these faithful friends continue to take their holidays working for nothing in some of the steepest vineyards in the area, and bring their sons and nephews too. For Mme Cotat looks like a lady who loves to cook. Not that she is large, but in talking of recipes her eyes light up, she becomes animated - it is a subject of passionate interest. For this group she pulls out all the gastronomic stops. Round this table there is friendship and feasting and in the cellars, serious tasting to be done.

When they come in from the vines, the Cotat's band of volunteers are revived by going straight down into the cellars for a glass, or two, or four, of wine from the barrel. They can confidently expect to sit down afterwards to an excellent meal of some favourite dishes, such as a well-seasoned salad of potatoes and herring fillets (see page 109), *coq au vin* flamed in *marc* (brandy distilled from the grape must left after the harvest) and simmered in Sancerre, followed by cheese and a dessert of caramelized *gâteau de rhubarbe* (see page 117). There are *ragouts* of mutton or rabbit, or stuffed tomatoes on other days (see page 37); an ox tongue is cooked like a *pot-au-feu*, slowly with lots of vegetables, and served with a Madeira sauce

White Sancerre from the nearby village of Chavignol

- another favourite (see page 116). On Sundays the lunch starts with a spinach tart (see page104), followed by a good shoulder of mutton which has been marinated in white wine, oil and herbs, larded with many slivers of garlic, then spit-roasted over an open fire.

A street in the walled town of Sancerre

A street away, still in the pretty little village of Chavignol, the ladies of the Bourgeois family have gone on strike. This is a large and well-known estate, making Sancerre and using between 50 and 70 pickers. In 1990 Mme Bourgeois announced that she and her helper were exhausted after years of cooking for the harvest - a new system must be found! Now most of the pickers are local people who go home after work, and these ladies, who look after customers in the attractive tasting-room and in the family shop on the main street, only cook in the evenings. There are still about fifteen pickers to be lodged and fed, as well as the vat-house workers.

Lapin au Sancerre is one of the best dishes here. The jointed rabbit is browned and simmered slowly in white wine with mushrooms for two hours, then potatoes are added in a layer on top about twenty minutes before serving (see page 115). All the usual *plats mijotés* - the long-cooking stews - which form the backbone of harvest cooking are in the Bourgeois repertoire as well as *des grillades* - grilled meat dishes.

Fruit compotes go well with the sweet biscuits made and sold in the shops here and known as *croquets de Sancerre*, or *lichous de Sancerre*, or with a *gâteau au vin blanc*.

Lunch at the Domaine aux Moines ➤

THE BIOTTEAU'S SOUPE A L'OIGNON

ONION SOUP

This is certainly not an elegant party soup, more to be enjoyed before going out early on winter mornings to do some energetic sport, or when coming home cold and tired and finding little in the fridge.

It has a soothing, almost medicinal quality (excellent if you are suffering from a cold).

FOR 6 PEOPLE

2 large onions
approximately 60 g (2 oz) butter
approximately 2 teaspoons plain flour
1 - 1½ litres (1¾ - 2½ pints) water
freshly ground black pepper

Peel and chop the onions finely. Brown them in the butter in a heavy-based pan. They must be well-browned, 'not burnt but almost,' says Mme Biotteau. In practice this means cooking them quite briskly, but not frying them to a crisp, for about 10 to 15 minutes, stirring from time to time. The onions begin to caramelize. This is important to give flavour, because no stock is being used. Stir in enough flour to be absorbed by the buttery juices to make a roux. This is the moment to start adding the water, a little at first to avoid making the mixture lumpy, then the rest. Bring back to the boil and leave to simmer for about 10 minutes. Season the soup well with plenty of pepper.

As can be seen, this is a very simple soup. The Biotteau family sometimes add a little of their own *vin doux*. There are no other additions, such as cheese and bread as in the famous *soupe à l'oignon* enjoyed in the early morning by porters at the old Parisian market of Les Halles.

TARTE AUX EPINARDS

SPINACH TART

In the village of Chavignol, famous for its white wine and goat cheeses, Mme Cotat's Sunday lunch for the harvesters begins with this tart, followed by a leg of lamb, spit-roasted over a wood fire.

FOR 6 - 8 PEOPLE

FOR THE PASTRY:

250 g (8 oz) plain flour
a pinch of salt
150 g (5 oz) soft butter
1 egg yolk
3 - 4 tablespoons cold water

FOR THE FILLING:

750g (1½ lb) fresh spinach, or 375 g (12 oz) chopped,
frozen spinach
2 tablespoons butter
1 large onion, peeled and finely chopped
salt and freshly ground black pepper
250 g (8 oz) fromage blanc or fromage frais
(you can use a low fat one)

3 eggs, lightly beaten
60 g (2 oz) freshly grated Parmesan cheese
150 g (5 oz) double cream
pinch of grated nutmeg

Preheat the oven to gas mark 4, 350°F, 180°C. Make the pastry in the usual way; use to line an 28 cm (11 in) tart tin. Bake blind for 15 minutes in the pre-heated oven.

Wash the fresh spinach and discard the stems. Blanch for five minutes in a big pan of boiling water. Drain, cool and squeeze dry with your hands. Chop roughly. If you are using frozen spinach you can omit this step and go straight to the next: melt the butter in a frying pan and cook the onion until soft. Add the spinach and let it cook in the butter for about 5 minutes, stirring to make sure it does not burn on the bottom. Add salt and pepper. Drain away any water which remains.

Off the heat, add the *fromage blanc*, the beaten eggs, Parmesan, cream and nutmeg. Mix all together and pour into the pastry case, spreading it evenly. Bake in the oven at the same temperature as before for 30 minutes, or until the pastry is browned and the filling has set. The consistency of the filling should be moist. Serve hot, warm or cold.

RILLETTES

POTTED PORK

Large bowls of this soft, melting kind of potted pork or pâté are in every charcuterie in the Loire. A fine example of the French talent for turning cheap ingredients into something delicious, it is easy to make at home.

FOR 8 PEOPLE
*1 kg (2 lb) belly or neck of pork, rind and
bones removed
500 g (1 lb) pork back-fat
1 clove garlic
bouquet garni of parsley, thyme and bay leaf
salt and freshly ground black pepper*

Cut the meat into short strips about the width of a finger. Cut up the back-fat coarsely. Put all into an ovenproof casserole with the garlic, herbs, salt and pepper and enough water just to cover the bottom of the pan. Cover and cook in a very slow oven - gas mark ½, 250°F, 120°C - for about four hours.

It cannot be said to look very appetizing at this stage. The next step is to drain off the fat and keep it. Throw away the *bouquet garni*. Pound the meat in a pestle and mortar for a few minutes. The meat is soft and the job is easy. Resist the temptation to use a food processor - it ruins the texture which should not be that of a smooth paste. Finally, take two forks, one in each hand, and pull the pork into shreds. You end up with a pale mushroomy-pinky-brown mass of meat marbled with deeper pink streaks. Taste for seasoning and adjust if necessary - *rillettes* should not be bland.

Traditional *rillette* pots are like rather thick, salt-glazed, earthenware mugs, but any earthenware or china pot or bowl will do. Whatever you choose, pile the mixture into it without pressing it down into a compact paste. Pour the reserved melted fat over the top.

Rillettes will keep for 2 to 3 weeks in a cool larder or fridge sealed by the fat (which is there to preserve rather than be eaten) and covered with foil. Remember to take them out of the fridge in good time before serving, so that they are soft, to spread on fresh bread and enjoy with a glass of Vouvray or other fruity Loire wine.

VARIATIONS ON CLASSIC DISHES

❖ *Harvest cooks use a lot of rabbit. To make this dish with rabbit, use 250 g (8 oz) of rabbit to 750 g (1½ lb) of pork and cook with the other ingredients as for the pork.*

❖ *For 'rillons', add an extra half kilo (1 lb) of belly of pork, cut into roughly 5 cm (2 in) chunks, to the pork and fat of the original recipe. Cook as before. When you come to drain the fat off and before pounding the meat, extract these chunks and let them brown in a hotter oven. Eat them hot with a purée of potatoes, or cold as part of an hors d'oeuvre, either way with plenty of mustard.*

OEUFS DURS AU GRATIN

GRATIN OF HARD-BOILED EGGS

This is a good dish to cook when you already have the oven on for roasting or baking. They make a nice first course.

FOR 6 PEOPLE
*7 eggs
1 tablespoon thick cream (crème fraîche if possible)
1 tablespoon grated Gruyère,
1 tablespoon chopped parsley
salt and freshly ground pepper*

Preheat the oven to gas mark 6, 400°F, 200°C. Put six of the eggs into a pan with enough cold water to cover. Bring them to the boil and cook for ten minutes. Plunge the eggs into cold water and leave to cool. Shell and cut the eggs in half lengthwise. Scoop out the yolks into a bowl. Lightly beat the remaining egg and add to the bowl together with the crème fraîche, Gruyère, parsley and seasoning. Stuff the eggs with this mixture and put them in a lightly oiled gratin dish.

They now need a final five minutes in the top of a hottish oven to brown.

Mme Laroche's pork terrine

MME LAROCHE'S TERRINE DE PORC

PORK TERRINE

Mme Laroche is busy in the vines and vat-house during the harvest. When it comes to lunchtime, she jumps off her tractor and goes into the kitchen only a short time before her small band of pickers come in to eat. It makes sense to have a terrine, made a few days earlier, ready in the fridge for the first course.

FOR 12 SERVINGS

500 g (1 lb) belly of pork, boned
1 kg (2 lb) lean pork
6 allspice berries
1 egg, beaten
2 tablespoons cognac
150 ml (5 fl oz) dry white wine
salt and freshly ground black pepper
caul fat, back-fat or slices of streaky bacon
to cover the terrine
bay leaf, optional

Preheat the oven to gas mark 4, 350°F, 180°C.

Mince the meat coarsely or ask your butcher to do it for you. The belly of pork should give enough fat to keep the terrine moist. Grind the allspice. Mix all the ingredients, apart from the fat or bacon, together in a bowl, making sure that the egg, cognac and wine are blended into the whole mixture. Season well.

Pack the mixture into a terrine, capacity about 1 litre (1¾ pints). You could use an earthenware or enamelled cast-iron terrine, or a meat-loaf tin which, if it has no lid, you will need to cover with two layers of foil. Caul fat, that thin lacy-looking fat, should be spread over the top. It is often difficult to obtain; if so, use either thinly cut strips of back-fat or streaky green bacon instead, although the latter will give a rather bacony flavour to the juices. The point is to use something that will help to keep the terrine moist. Put a bay leaf on top as a garnish, if liked.

Bake, with the lid on, in the preheated oven, for about 1½ hours. About 20 minutes before the end remove the lid and the covering fat, so that the top may brown a little.

Remove from the oven. Cover with a piece of foil or grease-proof paper, weight - you can use one or two cans of food if you have no measuring weights - and leave to cool. Once cold, remove the weights. It will improve if kept for a day or two before being broached and will keep about a week in the fridge. Any surplus fat will have solidified on top and can be easily removed.

Slice and eat with gherkins and some of the juices that have set to a jelly round the terrine.

BEURRE BLANC
BUTTER AND SHALLOT SAUCE FROM THE LOIRE

The Secher family in the Muscadet are a bit scathing about great feasts to celebrate the end of the harvest. 'It is not at the end you need cheering up; it's during the three weeks of hard work before the end!' says Jean-Yves. All the same, he admits to making 'a little gesture' on the last day of picking. His gesture is to go into the kitchen and make his celebrated beurre blanc sauce to go with a poached fish.

His quantities are for 10. It is rare to have too much of this delicious sauce, so even if you are a smaller party it is worth making a lot. Jean-Yves uses his own Muscadet and his own white wine vinegar. Use the rest of the bottle to drink with the fish.

In the Loire valley you can eat this sauce with the local fish in little restaurants alongside the river. Here we are rarely able to get the same varieties, but it goes perfectly with salmon, or with white fish such as turbot or halibut, as well as giving a boost to cheaper varieties if you so wish. If you do have any left over, a small spoon-ful stirred into scrambled eggs as they finish cooking is rather good.

10 small shallots
10 tablespoons good quality
white wine vinegar
10 tablespoons Muscadet
(or other good dry white wine)
approximately 400 g (14 oz)
unsalted butter, chilled

There are two stages to this sauce, neither of which take long, nor are they difficult. The first step is to prepare a good foundation, as Jean-Yves would say.

Take the shallots and peel them. Use a sharp cook's knife and chop them very finely. Elizabeth David says (in *'French Provincial Cooking'*) 'until they are almost a purée.'

Put them into a heavy enamelled cast-iron pan, or tinned copper pan, with the wine and vinegar. The object of the exercise is to cook the shallots until they are soft, at the same time reducing the liquid by boiling without a lid until you are left with very little moisture in the bottom of the pan. Jean-Yves would also say that 'the shallots must give up their oil' in this process. It is hard to be precise about the time this will take - 10 to15 minutes perhaps.

You could put the pan aside at this stage, as long as the shallots are kept warm. The second stage must be carried out just before serving.

Have the butter ready, cut up into chunks of about 30 g (1 oz) each, and keep it cool until you need it. About 10 minutes before you are ready to serve the fish, put the pan back over a very low heat and start adding the chunks of butter, whisking them in one by one. The heat must not be so great that the butter starts to melt, so be ready to move the pan off the heat from time to time. Instead of melting, the butter must do what the French call 'mounting' (*monter* is the verb); if you have not seen this happen it is rather hard to visualize, but it is easy to do as long as the pan never gets too hot - better to have it too cool and go very slowly. You should end up with a sauce the texture of thick cream. It is very delicious.

SALADE DE POMMES DE TERRE ET HARENGS FUMES

SALAD OF POTATOES AND SMOKED HERRING FILLETS

Very suitable for hungry harvesters, this robust salad should be followed by something light. Alternatively, it makes a good, simple lunch, followed by fruit.

FOR 6 PEOPLE AS A FIRST COURSE

1 kg (2 lb) small waxy-fleshed potatoes
salt and freshly ground black pepper
1 medium onion
1 can or vacuum pack smoked herring
fillets (about 200 g/7 oz)
handful of fresh parsley

FOR THE VINAIGRETTE:

wine vinegar
walnut oil
groundnut oil

Smoked fish adds strong flavours to a dish

Wash the potatoes and boil in salted water. They should remain firm but cooked through.

While they are cooking, make the vinaigrette. One tablespoon of vinegar to three of oil is a fairly standard proportion for this kind of thing, but it is a matter of taste. It is usually more vinegary than a dressing for a green salad. The proportion of oils used would probably be two tablespoons of the cheaper groundnut oil to one of the expensive walnut oil.

Drain the potatoes and allow to cool until you can handle them. Peel them. Put them, the bigger ones cut in two, into a salad bowl - most French families have plain white ones in various sizes. Pour over the vinaigrette and toss the potatoes in it while they are warm. Add salt and plenty of pepper.

Peel the onion and chop it finely. Mix it with the potatoes.

Drain any liquid from the herring fillets, cut them into smallish pieces and mix with the potatoes.

Wash, dry and finely chop the parsley, then add to the bowl. This salad rather needs the bright green as the colours are dull. It can be served while the potatoes are still warm, or left to absorb more of the flavours of the vinaigrette and served at room temperature.

VARIATIONS ON CLASSIC DISHES

❖ *The smoked herring fillets are available in most French supermarkets, but if you cannot get them there are other versions: kipper fillets (preferably oak-smoked) work well. Hard-boiled eggs and tinned anchovies make another good partnership with the potatoes.*

❖ *Shallots or red onions can be used - there should be plenty of them in proportion to the other ingredients.*

❖ *Vinaigrettes for this vary from family to family. A 'false mayonnaise' (very mustardy vinaigrette) is a favourite in this salad of strong tastes. Starting with a good tablespoon of Dijon mustard, about 150 ml (5 fl oz) of groundnut oil is stirred in with a wooden spoon or a whisk, drop by drop at first, as for a mayonnaise. A few drops of lemon juice or wine vinegar are added to taste. It does not hold together for very long, so it must be made just before you need it.*

BOULETTES DE PORC FROM THE SECHERS' KITCHEN

These are meatballs, or sausages without skin, made from fresh pork. Their cooking time is flexible, so they make a quick and easy lunch dish.

FOR 4 - 6 PEOPLE
1 onion
a good handful of fresh parsley
a little fresh or dried thyme
500 g (1 lb) minced pork, a mixture of lean and fat
salt and freshly ground pepper
plain flour
approximately 250 ml (8 fl oz) wine, optional

Preheat the oven to gas mark 4, 350°F, 180°C. Peel and chop the onion finely. Chop the fresh parsley and thyme. Mix onions and herbs with the pork in a bowl. Season with salt and pepper. Take a tablespoonful of the mixture and squeeze it into a ball with your hands, then roll it in flour. Put aside until all the mixture is used.

Arrange the meatballs in an ovenproof casserole (an earthenware gratin dish could be used) and add a little water, or if you have an opened bottle, some wine, just to cover the bottom. Bake them in the preheated oven. Their cooking time can vary to fit your schedule, but allow 45 minutes to 1 hour in a medium oven (or longer at a lower heat if it suits you), just making sure they do not dry up, especially if you are using an open dish, by adding a little liquid and if necessary covering with foil. If you use a casserole you can put the lid on for most of the cooking and take the lid off and raise the heat to brown them at the end for 10 minutes or so.

Instead of water or wine the Secher family like to use *eau de vie noyau*, a white spirit flavoured with kernels from the stones of fruit such as cherries; such a thing does not often come the way of the average cook, but it is an indication that one can be inventive in what one chooses to use.

ROTI DE PORC AUX TOMATES, OIGNONS ET POMMES DE TERRE
ROAST PORK WITH TOMATOES, ONIONS AND POTATOES

This is one of two pork dishes cooked by Mme Laroche at the Domaine aux Moines. In France pork is roasted without the skin. To those who feel that crackling is the main reason for cooking a pork joint, this will doubtless seem extremely perverse. But the skin is prized for other culinary uses - usually to enrich, with its gelatinous qualities as well as its flavour, daubes and other stews, and especially dishes in which the meat is served cold accompanied by the jellied cooking broth. The layer of fat just below the skin is used for barding lean meat (to keep it moist during cooking); in sausages; laid across the top of pâtés and terrines to stop them from getting dry, or layered with potatoes as in the crapaudine (see page 38). The butcher usually removes the bones from the joint and these can be thriftily added to a stock. The French housewife takes home a neatly tied-up joint with just a thin layer of fat on top to keep it moist. Thus the most is extracted from a loin of pork. It is not really worth making this dish unless you have a joint of at least 1.5 kg (3 lb).

FOR 8 PEOPLE
a 1.5 - 2 kg (3 - 4 lb) joint of loin of pork, boned, the rind removed in one piece, not scored as for crackling, a thin layer of fat remaining on the joint
salt and freshly ground black pepper
500 g (1 lb) ripe tomatoes
250 g (8 oz) onions
1 - 1.5 kg (2 -3 lb) potatoes

Preheat the oven to gas mark 4, 350°F,180°C.

Allow 30 minutes per half kilo (1 lb) for a joint weighing up to 2 kg (4 lb), add 20 minutes per half kilo (1 lb) for every half kilo (1 lb) over this weight. (See Jane Grigson's *'Charcuterie and French Pork Cookery'* for this and other comprehensive information.) Tie the pork up in a neat shape, if the butcher has not already done this, and rub all over with salt and pepper. Put the joint on a rack in the roasting pan and bake in the preheated oven for the appropriate time.

Skin the tomatoes - try to get ripe ones - and cut them up roughly. Peel the onions and chop them roughly. Peel the potatoes if you like. If not, just wash them. Large potatoes should be cut up, small ones left whole. An hour before the joint is cooked, add the potatoes to the pan and let them cook in the fat from the joint. About half an hour before serving, add the onions and tomatoes to the pan. If the pork has given off a lot of fat, it is worth at this stage, that is just before adding the onions and tomatoes, spooning some of it off into a bowl to be used at another time to fry potatoes or *croûtons*.

Slice the joint - easily done since it has been boned - and arrange on a dish with the potatoes and the tomatoes and onions.

VARIATIONS ON CLASSIC DISHES
❖ *This is a dish which could be pot-roasted if more convenient, in a heavy casserole over a low heat. Brown the joint on all sides first, before putting on the lid and simmering gently. Add the vegetables as before and finish cooking uncovered.*

ROTI DE PORC EN CROUTE
ROAST PORK IN PUFF PASTRY

In Mme Laroche's second version she wraps the joint in puff pastry and serves it with whole garlic cloves and 'quantities of chips'. This is one of those happy dishes which create an enormous effect for relatively little work.

FOR 8 PEOPLE
*a 1.5 - 2 kg (3 - 4 lb) joint of loin of pork,
boned and prepared as above
2 - 3 tablespoons butter
Dijon mustard
500 g (1 lb) puff pastry (frozen can be used)
1 egg
2 - 3 heads of garlic*

Preheat the oven to gas mark 6, 400°F, 200°C.

Brown the joint on all sides in the butter. Set aside until it has cooled a little, then spread with Dijon mustard.

Roll out the pastry into a rectangle. It must not be too thin or it will burst during the cooking, letting out the juices. Place the joint on top and fold the pastry over quite loosely to make a parcel. Wet the edges with water and press them together. Trim off any extra. This can be used to decorate - cut out leaf shapes or anything else you fancy, wet one side and stick on.

Lightly beat the egg with a little water. Brush over the pastry to give it a nice shiny finish.

Carefully lift the parcel onto a lightly oiled baking sheet. Loosely cover the top of the pastry with foil or greaseproof paper to stop it browning too quickly; you can remove this towards the end of the cooking if you think it is not brown enough. Bake in the preheated oven for about 2 hours, turning down the heat to about gas mark 4, 350°F,180°C after 30 minutes.

In the meantime, separate the cloves of garlic but do not peel them. Blanch them in boiling water for five minutes. Bake them in the oven round the pork for the final 45 minutes. Make sure everyone who likes garlic gets their fair share to squeeze out of the skins onto their slices of pork. The splendid-looking, golden-brown, pastry parcel can be carved at table.

Pintade aux fruits d'automne - guinea-fowl with autumn fruit

PINTADE AUX FRUITS D'AUTOMNE
GUINEA-FOWL WITH AUTUMN FRUIT

This dish of roast guinea-fowl with apples and dried fruit is a favourite with the harvesters chez Cotat in Chavignol. The guinea-fowl makes a splendid sight on a nice dish, surrounded by the prunes, raisins, and apples with the melted redcurrant jelly.

FOR 4 PEOPLE
*approximately 300 ml (½ pint) stock
(chicken stock would be suitable)
20 prunes
125 g (4 oz) raisins
4 dessert apples, such as Russets
1 onion
butter
1 guinea-fowl, with liver if possible
125 g (4 oz) sausagemeat
salt and freshly ground black pepper
1 egg, beaten
2 tablespoons redcurrant jelly*

Preheat the oven to gas mark 4, 350°F, 180°C.

Heat the stock in a pan and add the prunes and raisins. Simmer for 10 minutes, then strain, keeping the stock on one side.

Chop the onion very finely, or mince it. Brown it in a pan in a little butter. Stone 6 of the prunes, chop them roughly and put them into a bowl with one of the apples, peeled, cored and cut up into small pieces, and half the raisins.

Add the minced liver of the guinea-fowl if available, the sausagemeat and the prepared fruits. Season with salt and pepper. Cook gently for 10 minutes.

Now add a little of the stock to moisten it. Take off the heat and allow to cool slightly before adding the beaten egg to the mixture. Stuff the guinea-fowl and sew up the vent.

Heat some more butter in an ovenproof casserole and brown the bird on all sides. When it is browned, season with salt and pepper and add a large glass of the reserved stock. Cover and leave to simmer in the preheated oven for about an hour. The juices are apt to caramelize on the bottom of the pan, so it is best to keep an eye on it and add a little more stock if necessary.

Core and cut the remaining apples in half horizontally. Bake them in their skins, cut side up, in a buttered dish in the oven for about 30 minutes, loosely covered with a piece of buttered foil.

Fifteen minutes before the guinea-fowl is ready, add the remaining prunes and raisins to the casserole.

Place the guinea-fowl on a serving dish, surrounded by the prunes, raisins and baked apples. Melt the redcurrant jelly over a low heat, then spoon over the baked apples.

PINTADE AUX POMMES ET MARRONS
GUINEA-FOWL WITH BAKED APPLES AND CHESTNUTS

Guinea-fowl are raised on many of the farms in the Loire and dishes made with them are often on harvest menus. Baked apples and chestnuts, both being in season at the time of the vendange, are a popular accompaniment.

For pintade aux pommes et marrons, apples are cored and baked in their skins in a buttered tin in the oven. (A variety such as Russets keep their shape. In any case they should be dessert apples, not cookers such as Bramleys.) Chestnuts are peeled, blanched and added to the roasting tin, round the guinea-fowl, which is cooked as above. Tinned ones are thought to be acceptable if there are no chestnut trees on the property, but even better are the vacuum-packed, ready-to-use chestnuts available from Italian specialty shops.

RAGOUT DE CANARD

DUCK STEW

This is a simple and rustic dish suitable for hungry harvesters.

FOR 4 - 6 PEOPLE

1 duck, weighing at least 2.5 kg (5 lb)
butter (as Mme Biotteau says, they use a lot of
butter in the cooking in this area)
a little plain flour
bouquet garni of thyme, parsley,
bay leaf and a stick of celery
12 shallots, peeled
1 kg (2 lb) potatoes

Cut up the duck, and brown the pieces in butter in a large pan. When they are well-browned, sprinkle with flour and stir to make a *roux*. Add enough water to cover, scraping the bottom of the pan to incorporate the *roux*. Add the *bouquet garni* and shallots. Bring just to the boil, cover and leave to simmer very gently for about two hours. After one hour add the potatoes, peeled and cut into even sized pieces.

VARIATIONS ON CLASSIC DISHES

❖ *One or two refinements can be made. First, the duck will give off quite a lot of fat and most of it can be poured off before adding the flour. (It could be used to fry some potatoes on another occasion, giving them an excellent flavour.) Secondly, the amount of flour could be reduced.*

❖ *To make a more elegant version, eliminate the flour altogether and use chicken stock instead of water. In this case, keep the pieces of duck and potatoes warm at the end of the cooking, remove the bouquet garni and boil the stock for about five minutes to reduce it a little and give it a depth of flavour and better consistency. Check the sauce for seasoning and reunite with the carved duck and potatoes.*

POULET ANGEVINE

CHICKEN WITH ONIONS, MUSHROOMS AND CREAM

The wine used for this dish would be local. Something from the area around Angers, such as a Sauvignon de Touraine or, from slightly further afield, a Muscadet, would be suitable and these wines are fairly widely available at a reasonable price. Plain boiled rice goes well with this dish.

FOR 4 - 6 PEOPLE

1 roasting chicken, weight about 1.5 - 1.75 kg (3 - 3 ½ lb)
2 tablespoons unsalted butter
12 small onions (as sold for pickling) or shallots, peeled
300 - 500 ml (10 - 15 fl oz) dry white wine
250 g (8 oz) button mushrooms
300 ml (10 fl oz) thick cream
salt and freshly ground black pepper

Cut up the chicken into 8 pieces (you can use the carcass and giblets to make stock for another dish). Melt the butter in a flameproof casserole just big enough to take the pieces of chicken in one layer with the onions fitting in between them. Brown the chicken pieces in the butter. Once browned, turn down the heat and cook for a further 5 to 10 minutes. Add the onions. Cover and simmer for 20 minutes. Add the wine, which should almost cover the pieces, let it come to the boil, lower the heat, cover and simmer slowly for 30 minutes.

Wipe the mushrooms clean and quarter any large ones. Add to the casserole, basting with the liquid. Simmer for another 10 minutes.

Now remove the chicken, onions and mushrooms with a slotted spoon or skimmer and keep warm in a dish deep enough to allow you to pour the sauce over to serve.

Boil the wine and cooking juices hard to reduce by about half and concentrate the taste. Check frequently, taste after 5 minutes and thereafter until it seems right, remembering that the taste will be diluted by the cream.

Add the cream and simmer for a few minutes to heat through. Taste and season. Pour over the chicken and serve.

LAPIN A LA MOUTARDE
RABBIT IN MUSTARD AND CREAM SAUCE

In the simplest version of this family dish, the jointed rabbit is spread with mustard and roasted in the oven for 30 minutes - at the end cream is added to the roasting pan to make the sauce. The method varies from family to family. Mme Laroche's version follows.

FOR 4 PEOPLE
**l large rabbit, jointed
60 g (2 oz) butter
Dijon mustard
1 glass of cognac, about 125 ml (4 fl oz)
salt and freshly ground black pepper
dried thyme
200 g (7 oz) pot of crème fraîche**

Preheat the oven to gas mark 3, 325°F, 160°C.

Brown the rabbit joints in the butter in an enamelled cast-iron casserole. This needs to be done over quite a high heat to sear the outside of the meat and seal in the juices, otherwise the rabbit will be dry. When they are browned, smear them quite thickly with Dijon mustard. Warm the cognac in a little pan. Pour it over the rabbit in the casserole and light carefully with a match. When the flames have died down, add salt, pepper and a pinch or two of dried thyme. Bake in the preheated oven, covered, for about 40 minutes.

Remove the casserole from the oven and put it back over a gentle heat on top. Stir the cream into the cooking juices. Let it simmer for five minutes, turning the pieces of rabbit in the sauce. Taste and adjust the seasoning. Plain boiled rice is often served with this dish.

MME BOURGEOIS LAPIN AU SANCERRE
RABBIT COOKED IN SANCERRE

Recipes similar to this are used in most wine-making areas, using the local wine. Although it cooks for a long time, the preparation time is short; an added advantage is that it is all cooked in one pot, from which it is served.

FOR 6 PEOPLE
**250 g (8 oz) mushrooms, button or flat as available
1 large rabbit, jointed
1 onion, peeled and thinly sliced
1 tablespoon butter
½ bottle dry white wine, Sancerre if possible
bouquet garni
salt and freshly ground black pepper
12 small potatoes**

Prepare the mushrooms by wiping them clean; leave them whole if they are button mushrooms, quarter them if larger.

Brown the pieces of rabbit and the onion in the butter in a flameproof casserole. It is best to sauté the onion first and remove, then turn up the heat for the rabbit. When the rabbit joints have taken colour, deglaze the pan with the white wine, stirring and scraping the bottom of the pan. Now add the *bouquet garni*, salt, pepper, onions and the mushrooms.

Bring slowly just to the boil. Cover the casserole and let it simmer as gently as possible for 2 hours. This means that it is barely bubbling. It really must not go any faster or will be over-cooked and stringy instead of melting and tender.

Wash the potatoes and peel them if you like, but this is not necessary. If you cannot get small potatoes, you will have to use bigger ones and cut them up, but it is not so good as they tend to get mushy round the edges. Twenty or thirty minutes before the rabbit is ready, add them to the casserole to cook on top of the meat. When they are done, the dish is ready to serve. As you lift the lid of the casserole, a wonderfully appetizing smell reminds you how good these simple, rustic, simmered dishes - *plats mijotés* as the French call them - are.

LANGUE DE BOEUF POT-AU-FEU, SAUCE MADERE

OX TONGUE WITH MADEIRA SAUCE

Tongue, with this traditional sauce, is often served and much appreciated during the harvest. Dry Sercial is the most suitable Madeira to use but, failing that, a Bual or Malmsey, both sweet, could be used, reducing the quantity by half.

FOR 6 - 8 PEOPLE

1 fresh ox tongue, weighing about 2 kg (4 lb)

FOR THE SAUCE:

10 small shallots
250 g (8 oz) smoked streaky bacon in one piece
30 g (1 oz) unsalted butter
15 g (½ oz) plain flour
approximately 600 ml (1 pint) reserved stock
1 teaspoon tomato purée
4 tablespoons dry Madeira (see note above)

The tongue is cooked in exactly the same way as a piece of beef in a *pot-au-feu*, with the same vegetables - onion stuck with cloves, turnips, carrots, leeks, celery branch, garlic and *bouquet garni* but omitting the cabbage. Follow the method given in the Burgundy section (see page 32), but first the tongue must be scrubbed, and soaked in cold water for about two hours. As for the beef, careful skimming is essential, before the vegetables are added.

The tongue will be cooked in 2 to 2½ hours. Drain, reserving the stock, some of which will be needed for the sauce; the remainder can be used in soup. The soggy vegetables should be jettisoned. When the tongue is cool enough to handle, peel off the tough outer skin, which is usually quite easy to do. Cut away any fatty or gristly bits, and the little bones. Now the tongue is ready to be sliced.

To make the sauce, peel the shallots and chop coarsely. Dice the bacon into lardons, little chunks - there is no need to waste time taking off the rind, it is going to be sieved out after giving its flavour.

Melt the butter in a flameproof casserole and brown the shallots and the bacon in it. After about 5 minutes, sprinkle in the flour and stir. Add a little of the stock. Stir well, scraping the little bits off the bottom of the pan. As it thickens, add the rest of the stock, then the tomato purée. Bring to the boil, turn down the heat, cover and simmer very gently for 30 to 45 minutes.

Just before serving, sieve the sauce, then add the Madeira. Put the sliced tongue into the casserole with the sauce, making sure it covers it, and simmer until it is warmed through.

Transfer, if you wish, to a more elegant dish. Any extra sauce can be handed round in a sauce-boat. Serve with rice.

VARIATIONS ON CLASSIC DISHES

❖ *The flour to stock ratio is really a matter of taste. Many people prefer to eliminate flour from their sauces as far as possible and might like to reduce the amount given here and have a thinner sauce. The quantity of Madeira is likewise a matter of individual taste. The thing to do is taste the sauce after adding a spoonful and adjust accordingly. You can then also add salt and pepper as needed.*

❖ *Madeira is a fortified wine: a medium-sweet sherry could be used instead.*

MME COTAT'S GATEAU DE RHUBARBE
CARAMELIZED RHUBARB CAKE

This cake is equally good made with sliced apples, pears, apricots, pineapple, blackberries or cherrries.

FOR 6 PEOPLE
5 heaped tablespoons plain flour
4 tablespoons caster sugar
3 tablespoons milk
2 tablespoons cooking oil (a light olive or
sunflower oil would be suitable)
1 egg
1 teaspoon baking powder
750g - 1 kg (1½ - 2 lb) rhubarb, trimmed and
cut into short equal lengths

FOR THE CARAMEL SAUCE:
125 g (4 oz) sugar
90 g (3 oz) butter
1 egg

Preheat the oven to gas mark 8, 450°F, 230°C.

Mix all the ingredients, except the fruit, together in a bowl to make quite a soft, almost runny, dough.

Butter a 23 cm (9 in) round sponge tin. Sprinkle with flour. Spread the mixture into it. Place the rhubarb pieces on top of the mixture.

Bake in the preheated oven for about 30 minutes, until golden. (It will rise a little.)

Meanwhile, prepare the caramel sauce. Melt the sugar and butter together in a small pan. Remove from the heat, cool a little, then stir in the egg.

When you take the cake out of the oven, pour this sauce over it. Put it under a hot grill for two minutes or until the sauce has caramelized. Watch it carefully, as it burns easily. Leave the cake to cool. It may be eaten warm or cold.

GATEAU AU VIN BLANC
WHITE WINE CAKE

This simply-made cake is good with compotes, vanilla custard, crème Chantilly or sliced and spread with jam or chocolate. Quantities are given as a volume as well as weight. In France, mustard is often sold in tumblers which can be used for wine or water afterwards and these are commonly used as a cooking measure. They hold about 60 g (1½ - 2 oz) or 100 ml (3½ fl oz).

FOR 4 PEOPLE
3 eggs
250 g (8 oz) caster sugar
1 pinch of salt
grated zest of 1 lemon
¾ glass of sunflower or groundnut oil/75 ml (2½ fl oz)
1 glass dry white wine/100 ml (3½ fl oz)
3 glasses plain flour/175 g (6 oz)
1 teaspoon baking powder
butter for greasing

Preheat the oven to gas mark 5, 375°F, 190°C.

Butter a 23 cm (9 in) sponge tin or small charlotte mould.

Beat the eggs, sugar, salt and lemon zest together until white. Add the oil and wine and continue beating for two more minutes. Sift the flour and baking powder together and incorporate into the mixture.

Pour into the tin and bake in the preheated oven for about 40 minutes. Turn out of the mould onto a cooling rack.

Tarte aux poires - pear tart

TARTE AUX POIRES
PEAR TART

Mme Laroche makes two different pear tarts. The first is made very simply, using a sweet flan pastry (pâte sablée), rolled out to line a removable-base tart tin; the peeled, cored and sliced pears are then arranged in circles on the pastry and the whole is baked in the oven. This allows the taste of the pears to be appreciated, using the sweet, biscuity pastry as a foil. There are more elaborate versions, in which cream or a crème pâtissière is poured over the pears before baking, and very often ground almonds are used in the sauce - these are all delicious in their way, but more the sort of thing for a party than a good everyday family dish.

If things are going smoothly in vineyard and cuverie and she has time, Mme Laroche makes this more unusual tart in which the pears are first marinated, then enclosed in puff pastry (pâte feuilletée).

FOR 6 - 8 PEOPLE
750 g (1½ lb) ripe dessert pears

FOR THE MARINADE:
60 g (2 oz) caster sugar
a little freshly ground black pepper
4 tablespoons cognac

FOR THE TART:
500 g (1 lb) frozen puff pastry, ready to use
1 egg
a little extra caster sugar

Peel and core the pears. Slice finely and put into a bowl. Sprinkle with the sugar and cognac. Grind a little black pepper over them. Turn them in this mixture from time to time and leave to marinate for 2 to 3 hours.

Roll out the pastry. Butter a 24 cm (9½ in) tart tin. Line it with the pastry, keeping aside enough to make the lid later. Chill the pastry-lined tart tin in the fridge for 30 to 60 minutes.

Put a heavy baking sheet in the oven and preheat to gas mark 7, 425°F, 220°C.

Lift the pears out of the marinade with a skimmer and arrange on the pastry base. Keep the marinading liquid to use when the tart is baked. Use the remaining pastry to make a lid. Wet the edges with water and press together to seal. Use any trimmings to cut shapes and decorate the lid, sticking them on with a little water. Prick the lid with a fork several times.

Break the egg into a bowl and beat lightly. Brush this over the lid. Shake some sugar over it and bake in the preheated oven on the baking sheet for 20 minutes.

The marinade can be served in a jug and Mme Laroche usually serves a bowl of thick *crème fraîche* with the tart.

SALADE VIGNERONNE
SALAD OF GRAPES AND APPLES IN SWEET WHITE WINE

The grapes used for this are sweet table grapes, although the Chasselas used to be widely planted round Pouilly-sur-Loire, making white wine for everyday consumption. Now they have largely been replaced by Sauvignon Blanc and the Chasselas is grown as a table grape further south.

FOR 4 PEOPLE
150 g (5 oz) white Chasselas grapes
150 g (5 oz) black Muscat grapes
2 Cox's apples
90 g (3 oz) caster sugar

250 ml (8 fl oz) sweet white wine (vin doux) such as Coteaux du Layon, (or it could be a Sauternes or Barsac)

Wash the grapes and pat them dry, take them off the stalk. If you have time to take the pips out it will make a more elegant salad.

Peel and core the apples. Slice them finely.

Put the grapes and apples in a shallow bowl, sprinkle with sugar and shake the bowl to mix the fruit and sugar together. Pour over the wine and keep in the fridge till ready to serve.

CHAMPAGNE

Synonymous with celebration, champagne is the world's favourite party wine - that is, for those who can afford it. But until approximately the middle of the nineteenth century the textile trade was as important as wine to Rheims, the great cathedral city which is the commercial centre of the champagne trade. It was in the eighteenth century that sparkling champagne became popular at the court of the Regent, Philippe Duc d'Orléans; then later, Mme de Pompador, who is supposed to have held that champagne is 'the only wine that leaves a woman beautiful after drinking it,' gave it the seal of her approval. It has been drunk by the rich and famous ever since.

◄ *A view over the chalky vineyards of Champagne*

*U*nlike most other wine-growing areas of France, in Champagne few growers vinify and bottle their own produce, perhaps because of the great expense involved in the special process known as the *méthode champenoise* (champagne method). It is estimated that about half the grapes grown in the Champagne region are sold by the growers to big merchants, firms with a world-wide reputation, such as Bollinger, Krug, Moët and Chandon, Mumm, Veuve Clicquot and Louis Roederer, who vinify them. The balance is vinified by large co-operative groupings of growers or individual growers, who mainly sell their champagne to French private customers.

Three main grapes are planted: Chardonnay and Pinot Noir (as in Burgundy) and the Pinot Meunier. It is a curious fact that champagne, which is mainly white (though sometimes pink) is made from two red grapes (the Pinot Noir and Pinot Meunier). The grapes are pressed almost immediately after they have been picked and the red colouring matter in the skins does not come into contact with the juice (unless a rosé champagne is being made when there will be brief contact).

Over the centuries Champagne has been the scene of many bloody battles. Now it seems rather peaceful, with fertile hectares given over to wheat-growing on a grand scale. Cemeteries and memorials to British, American and Commonwealth soldiers are a poignant reminder, however, of the area's recent tragic past during two Battles of the Marne in the First World War.

The vineyards are on rolling chalk hillsides (the same

Bottles of champagne on the mantlepiece at Roederer in Ay

The dining room at Roederer's premises in Ay with the stove at the far end lit to warm the pickers

band of chalk which makes the cliffs of Dover so famously white) into which have been carved hundreds of kilometres of cool underground cellars. These are crucial to the making of fine champagne, which undergoes a second fermentation in bottle during the spring following the autumn in which the grapes were picked and vinified. The carbon dioxide produced in this fermentation (which requires sustained cool temperatures) dissolves into the wine, giving the characteristic sparkle.

The Champenois have developed a method over many decades for removing the spent yeasts which have brought about this sparkle - they freeze the neck of the bottle which is held upside-down in a brine bath, having previously shaken the yeast deposit down onto the cork (a process known as *remuage*, which is translated as riddling); the deposit is trapped in the frozen bullet of champagne, so when the closure is removed, it is shot out by the pressure inside the bottle (*dégorgement* or disgorging).

The bottle must then be topped up and a proper champagne cork and its wire muzzle put on. It is easy to see that this process is a skilful, labour-intensive one, although it is now being increasingly mechanized.

Champagne is not normally sold with the name of its village or vineyard of origin on the label. Instead, the big Champagne merchant houses buy or grow their own grapes in many different communes and create their own blends. The region is divided into three districts: the Montagne de Reims, the Vallée de la Marne and the Côte des Blancs. Tradition has it that Dom Pérignon, a seventeenth century monk at the Abbey of Hautvillers on a hillside above Epernay (now one of the centres for champagne-making) first tasted and blended grapes from different villages to produce a perfectly balanced champagne. He is also credited with the first use of corks, which, after all, make sparkling champagne as we know it today, possible.

CHAMPAGNE AND CABBAGE

In her kitchen in Le Mesnil sur Oger - vineyards can be seen from the window - Mme Bernadette Emprin is making *boulettes* for her grandsons' lunch and talking about the harvests of her youth. *Boulettes* have not changed - delicious little 'bullets' of highly seasoned, minced meat - but the harvest has.

In her youth, she says, all the pickers were lodged and fed. It was essential; now it is becoming rare. The pickers left on foot for the vines early in the morning after a quick coffee. Everyone was given a *panier* (a basket to put the grapes in), a pair of secateurs and a goblet, attached to their belt when not in use, for the duration of the harvest - woe betide any harvester foolish and careless enough to lose any of their equipment - they would have to pay for it. At about 8.45 the *chef d'équipe* distributed a breakfast, which was eaten standing round a little fire of dry vineshoots, and consisted of bread, a piece of salami, liver pâté, brawn and maybe a piece of the local cheese, Maroilles (the traditional harvest cheese according to Mme Emprin). They were soon back at work.

The sight of the horse and cart arriving just after midday must have been welcome, for work went on whatever the weather. Lunch, unloaded from the cart, was eaten in the vines. One tin plate each served for soup and a slice of meat and a vegetable. If you wanted fruit, you picked a handful of grapes.

The evening meal hardly varied - one day *soupe aux choux*, one day *pot-au-feu*: good dishes in themselves but monotonous day in, day out.

So those were the good old days ... and the impression Mme Emprin gives is that you can keep them. Nostalgia is for those who did not have to do the work. Now Mme Emprin, a redoubtable lady and admired cook, is happy to help in the harvest kitchen of a nearby *vigneron* cousin, a member of the co-operative Union Champagne, where the atmosphere created by hard work and good meals is cheerful and cosy.

Soupe aux choux, otherwise known as *potée champenoise* (see page 132) and *pot-au-feu* (see page 32) are certainly on the menu. The *potée* positively bulges with a variety of vegetables and different cuts of salted pork and very often a large smoked sausage. In the *pot-au-feu*, the traditional assembly of meats is often augmented by a fine ox tongue, which gives the cook a chance to use the beef for *boulettes* or *hachis Parmentier* and to serve the tongue, sliced, with a Madeira sauce (see page 116) or fresh tomato sauce (see page 38) or with a cold vinaigrette.

There is, naturally, always a vegetable soup in the evening to start things off. 'Toujours une soupe le soir' is the unchanging refrain to the harvest songs which are the menus throughout French vineyard areas. Rare is the harvest household which has given up this particular tradition. Nobody seems to follow a recipe. One thing is certain, harvesters in Champagne, who are usually from the north of France, eat a lot of soup - three helpings can disappear in a trice.

In the evening, Mme Emprin might make potato omelettes to follow a good vegetable soup, then a green salad, cheese and maybe a traditional wine-maker's *tarte*

Mme Pompom carving roast beef

Boeuf mode being transferred from the Roederers' huge cauldrons to 'norvégiennes' which keep the food warm on its way up to the vines

aux raisins (grape tart) if it is an abundant crop but certainly not if it is a year in which the vines have suffered frost and only produced a small crop.

Another evening there might be a *salade au lard* (see page 131), a salad of dandelion leaves with hot bacon. The salad used to be made from the tender young leaves of dandelions growing between the rows of vines. Now, says Mme Emprin, the vines receive so many treatments (against mildew, oidium, grey rot, etc.) that there are none she would care to eat, so the leaves must be grown in the kitchen garden or bought from the local market. It remains a wonderful dish, with the slight bitterness of the leaves counteracted by the bacon and by a little red wine vinegar mixed with the melted fat given off in the frying, which makes the dressing for the salad. If dandelion is unavailable, curly endive can make a good alternative.

Another favourite country salad consists of potatoes (small long ones) sautéed with little bits of streaky bacon and onions, mixed with an escarole lettuce with a sharpish dressing and served while still warm (see page 131). These salads can make an excellent, simple lunch, with a piece of cheese and fruit to follow.

AN INDEPENDENT CHAMPAGNE GROWER'S HARVEST

Larmandier Père et Fils in the village of Vertus is one of the independent growers in Champagne who make and bottle their own wine and sell it themselves under their own label. The family owns about 9 hectares (22 acres) in Cramant and the champagne they make from this is particularly respected. They make several other *Grand Cru* and *Premier Cru* champagnes, as well as a small quantity of red wine - Côteaux Champenois-Vertus Rouge - something of a rarity. They export increasingly, but most of their wine is sold to private customers who like, as so many French wine-lovers do, to drive to the vineyards, taste in the cellars, make their choice and give their order directly to the person who made it, taking their case or two away with them.

It is the custom of the Larmandiers to assemble all their pickers the night before the harvest starts and to drink a glass (*une flute* - the tall champagne glass which shows off to perfection the beautiful sight of the rising bubbles) of their champagne together before sitting down to dinner. They are usually 35 to 40 at table, with about 24 being lodged.

The day starts with breakfast of coffee, tea or hot chocolate, bread, butter and jam, but a more serious breakfast is consumed in the vines at about nine o'clock, when there is a half-hour break for *charcuterie* and cheese and bread, which Mme Larmandier takes up to the vines herself. If the day is cold, there are hot drinks served around a brazier.

Game, such as wild boar and pheasant, are sometimes on the menu here, for M. Larmandier enjoys shooting. *Poulet au champagne, lapin au champagne* (chicken and rabbit respectively, cooked in champagne) and *potée champenoise* are among the local dishes. *Blanquettes*, roast pork, lentils with meaty little sausages, *boudins blancs* (white sausages made from a smooth-textured mixture of chicken or rabbit and pork, with cream, eggs and onions), chicory

wrapped in ham with a cheese sauce, are some of the other lovely French family dishes which are to be found here. Desserts include the ever-popular standby, *crème renversée* (caramel cream, see page 93), *clafoutis* and *tarte vite-fait aux pommes* (quickly-made apple tart, see page 139). At least once every two days, says Mme Larmandier with some pride, the pickers have a bottle of champagne with their meal. On Sundays at mid-day, the Larmandiers offer their pickers an aperitif of ratafia, a drink made like wine until the fermentation of sugars in the grape juice is stopped by the addition of *marc* or brandy. It is these little traditions, these extra attentions, different in each family, which create the atmosphere for which many pickers return year after year.

Labels from an independent Champagne grower

For many French people a festive meal must finish with a bottle of sparkling wine, champagne if possible, drunk with the dessert and/or little biscuits or brioche. For the end of harvest celebration dinner, known locally as *le cochelet* (most areas have their own expression), Mme Larmandier chooses a more elegant first course than usual, followed by leg of lamb and the dessert is usually ice cream flavoured with *marc de champagne* (local brandy) in the shape of champagne bottles, accompanied, naturally, by their own champagne.

Taking a break during the champagne vintage ➤

FEEDING THE 600 PICKERS
AT LOUIS ROEDERER

Mme Pompom has the quiet assurance of a military commander who has many successful campaigns behind her. For seventeen years she has been in charge of the entertaining by the prestigious firm of Louis Roederer at their property in Ay. Throughout the year customers from all over the world visit the vineyards and have lunch here. Mme Pompom fills the old house with flowers and makes sure that the food lives up to the enviably high reputation that the firm enjoys for its wine. The work is, in fact, part of a partnership with her husband, who started working in the vines here at the age of fourteen and is now *Chef du Secteur*, running this part of the Roederer estate. The pride they both feel in their work is evident. It is understandable. After all, the champagne that was the favourite of the Russian Tsars is, for many, quite simply the best. Cristal Roederer is a blend that was created for Tsar Alexander II in 1876 and its clear crystal bottle is still the epitomy of elegance.

The pickers' post arrives with lunch

Among the great champagne houses - many of whom are part of multi-national concerns - Roederer is one of the largest land-owners. It has remained a private, family-owned company and this certainly creates a different feeling. There are seven vineyard properties in the best villages, comprising 450 well-situated acres growing 75% of the grapes needed to make the 2.5 million bottles sold each year. During the harvest 600 pickers are fed and housed. The scale of the exercise is mind-boggling.

That the whole thing runs like clockwork is due to the efficiency of the ladies who are in charge of each of the seven harvest kitchens. Provisions are ordered centrally and delivered daily, with each of the cooks phoning in her requirements.

In the high-ceilinged old dining-room at Ay the wood-burning stove is lit and 90 pickers are sitting down to dinner. They badly need a hot meal. The weather conditions have been atrocious. The brightly coloured oilskins provided by the company have been in use all day, as showers drenched the vineyards. Lunch, *boeuf mode* (braised beef with carrots, see page 136) sent up to the vineyards in huge metal containers called *norvégiennes*, was eaten in the muddy fields under gloomy, grey skies.

In the kitchen Mme Pompom and her helpers know a morale-raiser is needed. They are sending out tureens of clear soup with vermicelli, to be followed by a rice salad with tomatoes, gherkins, olives, hard-boiled eggs and tuna fish (see pages 130 and 133). *Potée champenoise* (see page 132) comes next - the large, steaming plates of salt pork, smoked sausages and colourful piles of vegetables are bound to raise the spirits. By the time the locally-made Brie cheese is passed round everyone is feeling much better and the *tarte aux prunes* (open-faced plum tart) completes the transformation.

Lunch in the vines the next day is *lapin au champagne* (see page 133) with white haricot beans in plenty of butter and parsley, and cheese and fruit to follow. Again

to twenty eggs are prepared in a bowl for each table of eight. One woman beats the eggs, another makes the omelettes, another rushes them to the table in relays. They stand by to make more if anyone is still hungry. This is followed by big bowls of green salad and a fresh fruit salad to finish.

In the kitchen they are waiting for word that the vat-house workers are ready to eat. They are rarely able to leave the fermenting grapes at normal mealtimes and send a member of the team across the yard to warn the kitchen that they will be ready in fifteen minutes. Their work is crucial, they work long hours and the cooks are sympathetic, ready to spoil them with their favourite dishes and with plenty of cakes to keep them going when they are working late.

When they have eaten, Mme Pompom will get out her

Queueing for lunch in the Roederer vineyards on a rainy day

the weather is poor and the pickers' work made more difficult by the heavy mud underfoot. M. Pompom checks meticulously to make sure no leaves or mouldy grapes go to the vat-house.

The cooks are planning a dinner of warming onion soup with plenty of second helpings - these people from the Pas de Calais, northerners, do like soup - and omelettes. Tight organization is needed for this. Sixteen

carefully-planned list of menus and check that she has everything needed for the next day's lunch of *paupiettes de veau* (stuffed and rolled escalopes of veal, see page 135) with potato purée, cheese and fruit. It is lucky she only lives a few steps away as it is late before she leaves the well-ordered kitchen where the huge pots are clean and ready for the next day and it will not be many hours before she is back to supervise the 6.30 a.m. breakfast.

BOUILLON AU VERMICELLI

CLEAR SOUP WITH VERMICELLI

Soup, beautiful soup - without it the harvest would lose half its savour, even though the older generation holds that the younger generation does not seem to care for it in the same way. Maybe the truth is that in hot years soup seems old-fashioned and inappropriate and in cold years it is welcomed.

The jokes cracked about the soups in some establishments are as old and bitter as the ones about most school food, although I suppose the evening tureen very rarely actually does contain washing-up water. However, the frequently served clear consommé with vermicelli is rather open to abuse. If the consommé derives from an excellent pot-au-feu or poule au pot or some other such dish which results in a well-flavoured stock and has been carefully cleared of any fat, it will not be the butt of jokes.

FOR 6 PEOPLE
**1 litre (1 ¾ pints) well-flavoured
beef or chicken stock
60 - 90 g (2 - 3 oz) vermicelli or
other small pasta**

If the flavour of the stock is weak, you should reduce it by boiling hard until it tastes right, although if the original dish did not have enough vegetables and meat there is not much to be done. The stock should be carefully poured through a sieve lined with a muslin cloth and left to cool overnight. The fat will rise to the top and solidify and will be easy to remove.

Skim off the fat. Bring the stock to the boil and add the vermicelli (rice is sometimes used instead). Simmer for about ten minutes and serve.

VARIATIONS ON CLASSIC DISHES

❖ *It is an improvement to add some diced vegetables - carrots and turnips, or leeks for instance, at the same time as and in equal quantity to the vermicelli; some chopped fresh herbs such as parsley or chervil, or, if it is a chicken stock, tarragon or some leaves of sorrel, will transform this into a more elegant soup.*

❖ *It is an old habit to pour a glass of red or white wine into the serving of soup.*

POTEE CHOUX OR CHOUX AUX LARDONS

CABBAGE AND BACON

A cabbage dish, but rather confusingly, not the same thing as potée champenoise, described on page 132. At Roederer's they fill an enormous cauldron with cabbages when they make this vegetable dish for their pickers.

FOR 6 - 8 PEOPLE
**1 medium Savoy cabbage
250 g (8 oz) smoked streaky bacon in one piece**

Start by boiling the cabbage, quartered and cored, in water. While it is boiling for 5 to10 minutes you have time to remove the rind from the bacon and chop it into dice. Drain the cabbage well and chop it finely. Put a flameproof casserole over a moderate heat on top of the stove. Add the bacon and let the fat melt. Add the cabbage and mix it with the bacon. Stir for a few minutes over the heat so that the cabbage finishes cooking.

Serve it, as they do at Roederer's, with potatoes and pork chops, or as Mme Emprin does, with grilled sausages.

SALADE AU LARD
SALAD WITH HOT BACON

At the height of the nouvelle cuisine movement, warm salads were fashionable. They evolved from simple peasant salads like this and the one below. The preparation time is short, the flavours robust. Their success depends, not on culinary skill, but on buying good ingredients.

FOR 6 PEOPLE

1 bunch dandelion leaves or
1 head escarole or frisée lettuce
250 g (8 oz) green streaky bacon in a piece
red wine vinegar
black pepper

Wash and dry the salad leaves, then place them in a serving bowl. Remove the rind from the bacon and dice. (Thrifty French housewives will use the rind for enriching a stew or stock.) Let your frying pan get hot, then throw in the bacon - it sizzles and the fat melts. When crisp add to the salad.

Now quickly deglaze the frying pan with a little red wine vinegar and pour the 'dressing' - vinegar and bacon fat - over the salad, grind some pepper over it and eat while warm. Sad to say, a lot of bacon now gives off water rather than fat, in which case you are better off throwing this away and warming a little olive oil in the pan before deglazing with the vinegar. But when this dish is made with good bacon, the reception it gets makes it well worth going to the trouble of finding a source of supply.

SALADE DE POMMES DE TERRE CHAUDS, DU LARD ET DES OIGNONS
SALAD OF HOT POTATOES, BACON AND ONIONS

For this dish you need to track down some potatoes which the French use for salads because their texture is waxy, not crumbly. Some supermarkets now sell them - varieties such as Fir Apple Pinks, Kipfler or Roseval, which are small and long in shape.

FOR 6 - 8 PEOPLE

500 g (1 lb) potatoes
250 g (8 oz) smoked or green streaky bacon in a piece
1 medium onion, or several shallots
1 head of escarole or frisée lettuce
oil and vinegar
black pepper

Wash but do not peel the potatoes. Cut each into about four, depending on size. Dice the bacon, having removed the rind. Peel and chop the onion or shallots. Wash and dry the salad leaves, then place them in a serving bowl large enough to allow you to turn all the ingredients vigorously.

Heat a pan over a moderate heat and put in the bacon. Let the fat melt, then sauté the potatoes and onion in it. Keep stirring and scraping the bottom of the pan, so that everything becomes crispy without burning. If you feel the bacon has not given off enough fat, add some oil. The smell is wonderful and everyone will be very pleased to eat as soon as you mix the contents of the pan with the escarole dressed lightly with oil, vinegar and black pepper, ready in the serving bowl.

POTEE CHAMPENOISE

Potée, a sort of cross between a soup and stew, is rustic, comforting food. Colloquially it is sometimes called soupe aux choux. Many regions have their own version (some areas call it a garbure). Cabbage and salt pork are usually the essential ingredients. It is hard to give exact quantities - what follows is a guide - as everyone has his or her own preference about which vegetables, and how much of them, to include. This is the version that Roederer's Mme Pompom cooks for their harvesters.

Petit salé, sold in most charcuteries in France, is used in a number of rustic dishes and has an excellent flavour. It is a way of salting various different cuts of pork in order to preserve them; a dry salt cure is used, consisting of salt, saltpetre, sugar, spices and herbs. In this recipe the leaner end of the belly of pork is used, or a mixture of cuts if preferred, particularly if you are making it in a larger quantity. Use green streaky bacon in a piece or salted belly of pork.

FOR 6 - 8 PEOPLE
500 g (1 lb) salt pork ('petit salé' - see introduction)
250 g (8 oz) dried haricot beans
2 - 3 leeks
12 small or 6 medium-sized carrots
6 small turnips
2 medium-sized onions
bouquet garni made of 1 stick of celery,
2 bay leaves, a few sprigs of thyme (fresh or dry)
and parsley
1 large smoked pork boiling sausage, if liked
6 medium-sized potatoes, peeled
1 savoy cabbage
pepper

The first step, the night before, is to soak the joint of salted pork. Change the water several times. The dried beans also need to be soaked in water overnight.

Cover the pork with fresh cold water and bring slowly to the boil in a pan. Use a skimmer to remove the scum which rises as it comes to the boil. As in the method for *pot-au-feu*, this is an important step from the point of view of the clarity of the stock. Simmer for about 30 minutes.

Meanwhile, peel and roughly chop the leeks, carrots, turnips and onions into quite large pieces. Prepare a *bouquet garni*. Add the vegetables and herbs to the pork after the first 30 minutes, bring back to the boil and continue to simmer for another 30 to 45 minutes.

Drain the haricot beans and bring them to the boil in fresh water. Cover and simmer until nearly done - about 45 minutes, but best to test for yourself. Drain them and finish their cooking in some of the meat and vegetable stock. You are going to need some for cooking the potatoes also, so ladle out enough for both vegetables.

Boil the sausage in water for about 45 minutes.

Cut the potatoes into even sizes and cook in the stock.

Quarter and core the cabbage and boil in water separately.

It sounds as if a miracle of organization must be achieved, but in fact, exact timings are not very important. In many households all the ingredients are added, at intervals, to the same pot, thus saving a lot of washing-up. Unfortunately, the cabbage (and the smoked sausage if included) tend to overwhelm the other flavours and the stock is more or less unusable for soup for another meal. It is hard to judge the cooking time of the potatoes and haricot beans if they are included in the general melée of vegetables in a large pot and although it does not really matter if they disintegrate, you end up with a mushy purée which thickens the stock. It may sound rather a fiddle to have different ingredients cooking in separate pots (and the washer-up may complain), but it does result in a finer *potée*.

Mme Pompom serves the meat on one plate, the vegetables and sliced sausage on another. Cooking for smaller numbers, one simply assembles all the vegetables and meats, with one or two ladles of the stock, in one splendid, steaming dish. Put a pot of Dijon mustard on the table.

SALADE DE RIZ AU THON

RICE SALAD WITH TUNA

This old favourite turns up everywhere during the harvest. It varies from a simple tomato and rice salad - excellent if both the tomatoes and rice are top quality and good olive oil used - to more complicated versions. Some people always add shallots, others insist on plenty of fresh parsley, or chives; some make a mustardy dressing using an inexpensive oil, such as groundnut or sunflower, others a vinaigrette from a fruity olive oil and lemon juice.

FOR 6 - 8 PEOPLE
375 g (12 oz) white long-grain rice
olive oil and wine vinegar for vinaigrette
salt and freshly ground black pepper
3 hard-boiled eggs
500 g (1 lb) tomatoes
a few small gherkins
125 g (4 oz) green or black olives
1 medium sized tin of tuna, preferably in olive oil

Boil the rice as directed on the packet, or using your normal method, and taking care not to overcook. Drain thoroughly and mix immediately with a vinaigrette in a serving bowl. Season well with salt and pepper and leave to cool. This can be done ahead of time.

Shortly before the meal, shell the eggs and core the tomatoes. Slice the eggs, tomatoes and gherkins. Break up the tuna into chunks. Carefully fold all the ingredients, including the olives, into the rice salad and serve.

MME POMPOM'S LAPIN AU CHAMPAGNE

RABBIT IN CHAMPAGNE

No-one is going to buy a bottle of champagne just in order to use a glass in a rabbit stew. Mme Pompom has the use of ends of bottles left over from tastings, no doubt, and is simply making economic use of them. But if you plan to have a bottle of champagne, you could consider appropriating a glass for the kitchen - it makes a wonderful dish! Or you could substitute a glass of dry white wine. Similarly, if rabbit is hard to come by, this method works well for chicken.

FOR 6 PEOPLE
1 large rabbit, jointed
1 tablespoon butter
12 small onions or 1 medium onion
1 tablespoon plain flour
1 glass of champagne
thyme
bay leaf
salt and freshly ground black pepper

Place the butter in a flameproof casserole over a medium heat and brown the pieces of rabbit in it well.

Add the peeled onions (if you cannot get small pickling-type onions, use a finely sliced, medium onion). Sprinkle with flour, turning the pieces of rabbit so they are well coated and the flour browns.

Add a glass of champagne, stirring as it bubbles, in order to deglaze the pan. As the flour and wine thicken, add enough water to barely cover the meat. Add a pinch of dried thyme, or several sprigs if it is fresh, and a bay leaf, salt and pepper. Cover and simmer slowly for about an hour until tender. Serve with steamed potatoes or rice.

Potage aux cinq légumes, vegetable soup and paupiettes de veau, stuffed and rolled veal escalopes

MME POMPOM'S POTAGE AUX CINQ LEGUMES
FIVE VEGETABLE SOUP

Many and various are the vegetable soups made by harvest cooks, depending on what ingredients are in the garden or market. 'Bonne femme' (mainly onions, leeks and potatoes) and 'potage Crécy' (mainly carrots) are two old favourites among the thick soups. These creamy-textured soups do not need a stock base. In general, the peeled vegetables are chopped and sweated in butter, water is added, brought to the simmer and when the vegetables are soft but not sodden, the whole is put through a mouli-légumes or liquidized. Cream may be added or more butter and parsley is often sprinkled over at the last minute.

This unusual combination of vegetables gives an excellent, very fresh-tasting soup.

FOR 6 PEOPLE
**4 medium carrots
3 medium potatoes
2 medium turnips (the French purple
and white variety)
1 round lettuce
3 leeks
30 - 45 g (1 - 1½ oz) butter
1 litre (1¾ pints) water
salt and freshly ground black pepper**

Peel the root vegetables and wash the lettuce. Wash and trim the leeks. Chop everything roughly. Melt the butter in a pan, add the vegetables, cover and sweat for about 10 minutes. Add the water, bring to a simmer and leave to cook gently for 20 to 30 minutes. It is important not to overcook the vegetables.

Put through the medium blade of a *mouli-légumes* or liquidize: the soup should not have too fine a texture. Taste and add seasoning. Heat through and serve.

PAUPIETTES DE VEAU
STUFFED AND ROLLED VEAL ESCALOPES

The success of this dish depends on the quality of the sausagemeat. Make sure it has not been stretched with breadcrumbs or rusk. The best solution may be to buy some Italian sausages from a delicatessen and skin them.

FOR 6 PEOPLE
**250 g (8 oz) pure pork sausagemeat
salt and freshly ground black pepper
6 thin veal escalopes
enough pork back-fat to wrap up each of the
parcels of veal and sausagemeat
15 - 30 g (½ - 1 oz) butter
approximately 150 ml (5 fl oz) water
bouquet garni**

Season the sausagemeat well. Lay each escalope flat. Put a spoonful of the sausagemeat stuffing on each and roll up, tucking in the ends. Wrap each one in a piece of the fat to keep it moist during cooking and tie it up like a parcel with string. (In France, the butcher would do all this for you.)

Brown the parcels very well in the butter in a casserole into which they just fit. Pour away the excess fat before adding water and deglazing. It is easier to do this if you remove the veal to a plate, then replace it. Add the *bouquet garni*. Bring back to the boil, cover and simmer very gently - too fast and the meat will toughen - for an hour or slightly longer.

VARIATIONS ON CLASSIC DISHES
❖ *Two small improvements can be made to the basic recipe. One is to add some thyme to the sausagemeat; the other is to deglaze with a glass of white wine before adding the water.*

BOEUF MODE, BOEUF BRAISE

BRAISED BEEF

This traditional dish, ideal for feeding a large party, comes up in every wine region and in a good many other places too. The basic principle is that you take a cheap piece of beef and cook it very slowly with onions and carrots in wine, flavoured with herbs. It differs from a daube in that the beef is cooked in one piece, not cut up. It is more correctly called boeuf à la mode. It is sometimes known as boeuf à la cuillère, because it should be tender enough to cut with a spoon rather than a knife.

There are many recipes: Julia Child is definitive in her 'Mastering the Art of French Cooking' Vol. 1 (see page 156) and in 'French Provincial Cooking' Elizabeth David is very good on the cold version, in which calves' feet are cooked with the meat, giving natural gelatine to the stock. When cold, the meat is sliced and surrounded by carrots. The stock is allowed to cool so that the fat may be easily removed. It is clarified if necessary. It is then poured over the meat and carrots and sets to a rich jelly. It makes a wonderful sight - the dark jelly with the meat and orange carrots just visible beneath it - and wonderful eating. People are apt to exclaim over it. Like pot-au-feu, there are no strict rules. Harvest kitchens are busy places and the cooks are likely to simplify. Mme Pompom takes the piece of beef and browns it well; she adds her chopped onions and browns them; she adds some flour and stirs it in; then the wine is poured in and salt, pepper and a bouquet garni added; some water makes up the liquid and she adds the carrots and potatoes too, and lets the whole thing simmer gently for about three hours.

A version with more depth of flavour calls for the beef to be marinated in wine and herbs overnight. It uses stock as well as wine in the cooking. Basically you pays your money and you takes your choice - if you want a simple and perfectly pleasant dish, as cooked by Mme Pompom, follow her method; if you want something with

Boeuf mode ready to cook in an old-style cocotte

more flavour and finesse, it will need a bit more attention to detail.

During its cooking the meat will shrink, a point to bear in mind when calculating how much you need. It is certainly much better to cook a piece that is too big. Small pieces just do not lend themselves to long slow cooking. Left-overs can be used in several delicious ways, e.g. stuffed tomatoes, stuffed peppers, hachis Parmentiers, boulettes, or reheated as a miroton (see below). Extra stock, as long as it is unthickened, can be turned into a consommé and served with rice or vermicelli cooked in it, or with diced fresh vegetables (a mixture of carrots, turnips, celery, tomatoes, for example) lightly poached in it, with some fresh herbs added at the end (coriander can be a spectacular success, parsley is fine). These ideas are just jumping-off points, the sort of thing a French housewife might do.

If you would like to cook this for a party, you might like to know that for 40 people you would need 7.5 kg (15 lb) meat, 4 pigs' trotters and 3 bottles of wine.

FOR A HOT BOEUF MODE FOR ABOUT 10 PEOPLE

approximately 2 - 2 ½ kg (4 - 5 lb) joint of beef: rump, topside or silverside are appropriate, boned and, if necessary, tied up to make a neat shape
3 tablespoons pork fat or cooking oil
water or beef or veal stock
2 pig's trotters split in two, or 1 calf's foot split, to give body to the stock, if liked. If neither are available, you could use a piece of fresh pork rind
15 g (½ oz) cornflour or arrowroot, optional
1 tablespoon Madeira or port, optional
1 - 1½ kg (2 - 3 lb) carrots
30 small onions, often called pickling onions, if available

FOR THE MARINADE:

2 carrots, 2 onions, 2 celery stalks, 2 cloves garlic, all peeled and roughly chopped
bouquet garni of parsley, bay leaf and thyme
6 allspice berries
6 peppercorns
salt
1 bottle of red wine, neither too acid nor too tannic as these elements become concentrated in the cooking, perhaps a Gamay from the Loire or Beaujolais

Place the beef in a large bowl with the marinade ingredients. Turn the meat from time to time, when you remember and leave about 12 hours (overnight is usually most convenient, but you are not expected to rise from your bed to turn the meat).

If you wish to skip this step, assemble all these marinade ingredients ready to use in the cooking.

Drain and dry the meat. Heat the fat or oil in a large flame-proof casserole and brown the piece of meat well on all sides. (This is the point at which Mme Pompom browns her chopped onions, then adds flour.) Pour in a little of the marinade and deglaze the pan, scraping the bottom with a wooden spoon. Add the rest of the wine and the vegetables, herbs and spices. Make up the liquid with water or stock so that it reaches about two thirds of the way up the beef. Add the calf's foot or the trotters. Bring just to the boil. Cover and simmer very gently and steadily for about 3 ½ hours.

In the meantime peel and prepare the carrots and little onions. Cook them separately in a little of the stock taken from the pot. If you were to cook them in with the beef you would get a rather sweet and very carroty tasting stock for the sauce or next day's soup. Also, it is nicer to have these vegetables slightly crunchy and not soggy as they would be if cooked slowly with the beef.

When the beef is cooked, lift it out and keep it warm while you deal with the sauce. Mme Pompom thickens her sauce, as we have seen, by adding flour in the initial stages. Obviously, if you are cooking this in quantity for 100 or more, you want to avoid making sauces just before serving. Doing it on a more domestic scale, you can taste the stock and decide what it needs. Strain the stock and return to the pan. Do you want to put some aside as it is to make a soup? Do you want to reduce it, by fast boiling? Or do you want to thicken it with a little cornflour mixed with Madeira or port, as suggested by Julia Child? If so, beat in this mixture and simmer for 3 minutes. Does it need more seasoning?

Add the ready-cooked carrots and onions and simmer for a few minutes, while you slice the beef. Arrange the meat and vegetables on a dish, pour over the sauce and serve.

VARIATIONS ON CLASSIC DISHES

❖ *Beef Miroton. This is a way of using up beef from a pot-au-feu and it works well for left-over boeuf mode if you have both beef and stock. For half a kilo (1 lb) of sliced beef, take half a kilo (1 lb) of onions. Peel and slice the onions finely. Cook them very gently in 30 g (1 oz) of butter - do not let them brown - they should be soft and yellow. Add a scant tablespoon of flour and stir it in. Start adding some beef stock, stirring as you go, to make a sauce. You will probably need about 300 ml (½ pint) of stock. Lay the slices of beef in the sauce, put a lid on the pan and heat it through.*

Tarte vite-fait, quickly-made tart

TARTE SUISSE OR TARTE VITE-FAIT
QUICKLY-MADE TART

This obliging recipe cannot fail! As its name suggests, it is quick.
It is also economical.

FOR 6 PEOPLE

1 egg
3 tablespoons milk
2 tablespoons oil
(such as groundnut or sunflower)
5 tablespoons plain flour
3 tablespoons fine semolina
(you can find this in Italian stores)
1 pinch salt
1 teaspoon baking powder
2 tablespoons kirsch or other
fruit brandy, if liked

FOR THE FILLING:

500 g (1 lb) dessert apples or ripe pears
icing sugar for sprinkling

Preheat the oven to gas mark 6-7, 400-450°F, 200-250°C. Put a heavy baking sheet in the middle. Butter a 23 cm (9 inch) tart tin.

Peel, core and thinly slice the apples or pears. Put all the other ingredients into a mixer and blend, or beat all the ingredients with a whisk till amalgamated. Pour the mixture, which is quite a liquid dough, into the greased tart tin.

Spread the sliced fruit over the mixture in the tin - there should be plenty of fruit.

Bake on top of the baking sheet in the preheated oven for 15 to 20 minutes. Mme Larmandier says it is quite gooey, although if you forget it and cook it too long, it is still good. Just before serving, sprinkle with icing sugar - it can be eaten warm or cold and is good with cream or vanilla icecream.

An abundant choice of fruit at a local market

ALSACE

$\mathcal{A}$lsace is a good example of the importance of geographical location to wine. The influence of the Vosges mountains is paramount. Alsace is very far north in wine-making terms and without the favourable protection of the Vosges, these vineyards would not exist. The vines are planted on the east side, where they catch the rising sun. The soil is relatively dry, as the rain coming in from the Atlantic falls on the west side of the mountain range. Vines do not need a lot of moisture, in fact quite the reverse, as the grapes suffer from rot if they get too wet.

◄ *'Karrenbottlich', or cuves carrées, filled with grapes from the harvest in Rodern*

Early on a Sunday morning in autumn the market around the church of St Joseph in the city of Colmar is being set up. Stallholders are arranging mounds of dark red beetroot with their vivid green leaves and varieties of large, long radishes: black, red and snowy white; pale green stacks of kohlrabi contrast with little cream turnips, tinged with pink. Cardoons with their beautiful grey-green foliage take up a lot of room on one or two stalls. On another, a stallholder cuts a slice of pumpkin and displays it to show off the bright orange flesh. There are still-life arrangements here to rival the riches of Colmar's museum. One woman has brought wild mushrooms gathered in the forests and at the neighbouring stall her friend has some local farmhouse Munster cheese, which is very pale orange, quite unlike the commercial variety. A man at another stall has only a loaf of bread for sale, but it is 2.25 metres (7 ½ feet) long, weighs 23 kilos (over 40 lb) and it has been baked for four hours in a wood-fired oven. It has a blackened crust and cream-coloured crumb and is made from a mixture of wheat, barley and oat flour. People are soon lining up to buy a slice.

Leaving the city, the *route des vins* takes you through pretty countryside with lovely stands of trees among the vineyards and a succession of villages each more picturesque than the last. Two of the most famous of these, Riquewihr and Ribeauville, are much visited - the proximity of the border makes it a favourite with Germans - and the prevalence of souvenir shops all selling the same decorated Alsace pottery is a little tiresome. However, the charm of the ancient, narrow streets - in Eguisheim, for instance - and the almost dazzling displays of geraniums falling from every balcony, are extremely beguiling. Above all, the villages are neat and tidy - the only exception being the big bundles of sticks, haphazardly arranged and precariously balanced on top of church spires and the towers of municipal buildings;

these curious constructions are storks' nests.

It is not like any other part of France. Many people here speak Alsace's own language at home and French in public; local people are apt to refer to the rest of France as *L'Intérieure*, the Interior.

Delightful wrought-iron signs hang outside many shops and businesses illustrating their wares, often humorously. Pâtisseries sell *kugelhopf* and other local cakes. You can buy and eat the local savoury tart, *tarte flambée*, straight from the oven at mid-day and evening. The pas-

Slicing a gigantic loaf for customers in Colmar market

try is rolled out as thinly as possible and it is baked at high heat in a baker's oven before the bread goes in.

The dishes here make use of many of the typical northern European ingredients - but with a French touch - notably in *choucroute garni* (see page 150) and other pork dishes, and there are plenty of quite reasonably-priced places to eat them, together with a glass or two of local beer or wine.

Because it is so far north, little red wine is made here: a small amount of Pinot Noir is cultivated. But Alsace is famous for the aromatic, white grape types, which thrive in this climate, each of them giving very different styles of

Pumpkins in Colmar market

wine. Traditionally the wines are known by the names of the grapes, rather than by village or vineyard names. However, in the last ten years the finest vineyards have been identified and classified as *Grands Crus* and in the future we shall find the precise names of origin appearing more frequently on Alsace wine labels.

Riesling is intensely fruity, with lively acidity, and ages well. Gewürztraminer is spicy (*gewürz* means spicy in German) and is often round and soft to taste. It should not really have any residual sugar but it feels sweet on the palate because of its ripeness and low acidity. Tokay Pinot Gris (nothing to do with the famous Hungarian sweet wine) gives a full-bodied wine, sometimes described as slightly smoky in flavour. Like Gewürztraminer, the wine can be round, rich, ripe and low in acidity but not actually sweet. These are the grape types believed by the Alsace growers to be the best and known as *les cépages nobles*.

Any of these 'noble grapes' may be left to ripen on the vines beyond the normal picking time if the autumn is a fine one. When greater concentrations of sugar have been achieved by this extra ripening, late harvest wines, known as *vendanges tardives*, are produced. If the so-called 'noble rot' (*pourriture noble*), caused by the benign fungus botrytis cinerea, develops, then glycerol is produced as well as the aromas and flavours being changed and enhanced. These grapes produce luscious dessert wines, known as *sélection de grains nobles*.

Another very individual grape planted in Alsace is the Muscat. It makes a lovely aperitif. It is also recommended by local people as a perfect accompaniment to asparagus, which is cultivated here, and which is notoriously difficult to partner with wine. The problem for the consumer is that the name sounds confusingly like Muscadet, or Muscat Beaumes de Venise. In fact, Muscat d'Alsace is a bone-dry wine which is piercingly fruity, one of the grapiest of all wines. Smell it once and you will always recognize it, for it is just like the best hothouse Muscat dessert grapes - despite being dry, which is rather puzzling! The fact that sweetness and fruitiness are two different things is often demonstrated in Alsace.

In addition, the Pinot Blanc is widely planted and gives wine which is flowery, easy to appreciate and often excellent value. Sylvaner used to be an important Alsace grape but it is losing in popularity to Pinot Blanc, perhaps because the former can sometimes be rather neutral.

The wines of Alsace suffer from something of an image problem. This may date back to the time when, after the Franco-Prussian war and the French defeat in 1870, Alsace became part of Germany and production of its finest wine diminished in favour of volume production of cheaper qualities. But Alsace returned to France in 1918 and has been rebuilding its reputation as a fine wine area ever since. It is true, however, that they have not always helped their own cause by shipping wines for export with residual sugar and high sulphur content which can cause headaches.

A single vineyard Great Growth wine

Alsace wines are not cheap. However, the net result is that there are many fine wine-makers whose quality products are mainly ignored by those who buy and consume fine wine.

Until very recently, Alsace wines were fronted in export markets by merchant shippers, such as Hugel in Riquewihr or Trimbach in Ribeauville. They are both famous, fine old firms who have their own estates; they also buy in grapes to vinify at the time of the harvest and sometimes also wine made by other growers, which they then bottle. Now there is a growers' movement encouraged by consumer demand for authenticity - increasingly people like to be able to identify the producer and know the precise origins of the wine they are buying. There is also a strong co-operative movement and cellars like those in Turkheim are now major flag-bearers for Alsace.

Riquewihr viewed across the vineyards

People often ask how to match Alsace wine with food - all too often the consumer is not very adventurous in this respect and falls back on a tried and tested combination from other regions. This is understandable as good

A Riesling Great Growth label

A SOPHISTICATED NEW BUILDING AND
A DETERMINED GRANDMOTHER

In 1992, the Domaine Zind-Humbrecht built an impressive new office, vat-house, cellars and bottling facilities. Situated between Wintzenheim and Turkheim and surrounded by vineyards, it is a splendid modern building, proof of the growth in demand for fine wine bottled by the grower. The reputation of this estate has gone from strength to strength since Leonard Humbrecht married Ginette Zind in 1959, linking two wine families. They started on what became a great crusade to identify the best vineyard sites, often rescuing them from disuse and replanting with vine types that Leonard judged appropriate to the widely varying soils. This was a revolutionary approach to wine-making at the time. Their son, Olivier, is equally concerned with quality. He also has the distinction of being the first Frenchman to have passed the U.K.'s prestigious Master of Wine exam.

Washing the karrenbottlich (tubs specially shaped for transporting the grapes) ready for the harvest in Bergheim

Mme Zind, Olivier's grandmother, is now an elderly lady, but until 1990 when ill-health forced her to give up, she cooked for the fifty harvesters. Even now she insists on making soup daily for them and making the coffee which is served with schnapps at the end of the meal; the rest of the meal is bought in from a local caterer but one senses that she does not really hold with this innovation, adequate though she admits the food to be. She quietly but firmly declares her intention of taking over again as soon as she recovers her strength. She is proud of her soups, which always start with a good base of a stock made with marrow bones and vegetables. Other favourites are salad of potatoes with onions and little bits of crisp, fried bacon and parsley, served with smoked pork; *tourte* - a tart of flaky pastry filled with minced pork or beef mixed with breadcrumbs, onion and parsley and topped with a lid of pastry; a dish of red cabbage and chestnuts with pork chops, and of course, *choucroute garni* and *baeckaoffa* (see pages 150 and 153). As she describes these you get the feeling it will be hard for her family to restrain her from returning to the harvest kitchen.

TRADITIONAL RECIPES AND DANCING IN THE VINES

Vins d'Alsace. Pierre Freudenreich & Fils. De père en fils depuis 1653. A polished brass plaque in the wall, next to an archway in the charming main street of the village of Eguisheim, announces proudly that this family has been making wine here for over three hundred years. The archway leads to a flowery, galleried courtyard where a trailer of grapes is being unloaded into the vat-house. Up some wooden stairs Mme Freudenreich, helped by two married daughters, is busy in the kitchen, as she has been every harvest for the last forty years.

Lunch is served punctually at mid-day in the vines. At a quarter to twelve, the food is loaded into a small jeep backed up to the foot of the stairs. Mimi, one of the Freudenreich daughters, takes the steering wheel. An elderly man climbs in beside her - an ex-bank clerk, long retired, he has been coming to do the harvest for even longer than Mme Freudenreich has been cooking. Mimi's daughter gets back from school just in time to hop in among the pots and plates in the back, and they're off.

Alsace villages are usually either Protestant or Roman Catholic, not mixed. As this one is Catholic it is not a surprise to find a large Christ on the Cross by the road-side at the corner of the vineyard where the Freudenreich's pickers are just finishing their rows. A table and benches have been set up next to it. Mimi starts laying out plates and cutlery and other members of the family arrive to help. One brings a baby who is passed from lap to lap during the meal, happily trying a taste of this and that. Vegetable soup is ladled out, turkey escalopes in breadcrumbs are kept warm to follow it, and the pickers sit down in the sunshine. Neighbours driving by with truckloads of grapes hoot and wave.

The cheese - a local Munster - is on the table. A few leaves of salad are left in the huge bowl and Mimi is encouraging people to finish them. Some, following the local habit, are eating their cheese with potatoes rather than bread. One of the pickers fetches her accordion,

An impromptu concert in the Freudenreich vineyard

which has come up in the jeep, and sits on an upturned *hotte* (the grapes are emptied into these by the pickers when their baskets are full) to play. It quickly turns into a sing-song and one older couple get up and dance, to applause from the rest.

Among this small band of sixteen pickers many have been coming back for twelve, or in some cases fifteen or sixteen years. Their fidelity is in part to do with the food. Here they continue to cook the old-fashioned dishes of

joints and smoked sausages; there is *coq au Riesling*, (see page 151) which is chicken cooked in local white wine and usually served with the special Alsace noodles called *spaetzle* (see page 151). There is also the other celebrated local speciality, *baeckaoffa* (see page 153), a mixture of pork, beef and lamb, layered with carrots and potatoes, and cooked for at least three hours. The harvest menus, here as elsewhere, also include the range of country cooking such as *blanquettes*, *fricassés*, *boulettes* to use up left-

Mimi and Barbara Freudenreich-Ling taking lunch to the pickers

Alsace so suited to feeding hungry people working in the fields. There is red cabbage with apples (see page 149), cooked slowly for two hours and served with roast pork and potatoes; *choucroute garni* (see page 150), the Alsace version of *sauerkraut* - for which finely chopped cabbage is salted in a barrel so that it ferments slightly, then rinsed of salt, cooked in white wine and served with smoked bacon

over meat, and a good *purée rose* (pink purée) made by mixing potato and carrot in a smooth purée to serve with roasts (see page 150).

Included in the dessert repertoire are the classic floating islands, caramel cream, apple compote (see page 92) and the local plum tart (see page 154). No wonder pickers keep coming back here.

VENDANGES A LA CARTE IN RODERN

The harvest here in Alsace differs from most other areas in that it does not necessarily continue uninterruptedly for two or three weeks. Rather, it is a question of *vendanges à la carte*. It may start with several days in September, picking the Muscat grapes which ripen earliest - they need to be picked before they are over-ripe because otherwise the crisp acidity which balances the intense fruitiness is lost. In October, the later-ripening Riesling is picked. There may be a gap of three weeks before the *vendanges tardives*, usually in November, depending on weather conditions. Most growers find it convenient to use local people.

Mme Koehly is a formidable lady. Brought up in a family of wine-growers who also had a small merchant's business and a restaurant with rooms, she is used to hard work. She married her husband when times were tough for the Alsace *vignerons* and prices achieved for their wine were low. They were determined to succeed but it meant working long hours. They took no holidays. Everything they made was put back into the estate, to buy more land or to instal better equipment.

She remembers her mother making sure that the men working in the cellars got a good start to the day - there was soup, two fried eggs and a pair of Strasbourg sausages each for breakfast. At 10.00 a.m. there was a break for coffee and schnapps - it was the custom of the older people to pour some of their schnapps over a piece of bread and eat it. The real picking very often started only at 1.00 p.m. and finished at 5.00, so there was no need to provide a mid-day meal, just coffee and the inevitable schnapps at the start, 'and the old peasant women insisted on being given cigarettes,' remembers Mme Koehly. Everyone had a miniature barrel (*le tonnelet*) filled with something to drink to take to the vines.

A pig was killed to provide pork dishes for the evening meals at harvest time. Joints were salted or smoked, sausages made. *Boudins* (black puddings) sometimes burst

These small tractors are made to go between the vines, which are trained high

while they were being boiled. This was turned to good account as a soup, poured over toast.

The head, feet and lungs were all used to make a dish glorying in the name of *schweinspaper*. It does not sound very enticing and Mme Koehly admits that it is not much liked and hardly ever made in these more affluent days. One way of using the pig's head that has survived is called *presskopf*. After cooking, the skin and bones are removed, and the meat, with the tongue and ears, pressed into a mould. This is a kind of brawn, excellent when sliced and eaten cold with little gherkins, as a first course. The fillet of pork was, and still is, salted, then smoked to make *kassler*. This can be can be eaten cold, rather like raw ham, or roasted and eaten as a hot joint.

The Koehlys succeeded in building up an excellent estate in and around Rodern. Now they have handed over to their son, Christian. He is in the forefront of the growers' movement, energetically promoting the fine wines of Alsace at home and abroad, hoping to persuade gourmets everywhere to experiment by partnering meat dishes of all kinds with these wines, just as they do here.

CHOU ROUGE AUX POMMES

CASSEROLE OF RED CABBAGE AND APPLES

For this recipe, the Freudenreichs use a local brand of spirit vinegar, called Melfor, which is flavoured with honey and aromatic plants. In the absence of this, red wine vinegar seems the best substitute. The vinegar stops the cabbage losing its colour. It is best to make this in an enamelled cast-iron, stainless steel or earthenware casserole because vinegar reacts with aluminium. The dish improves with re-heating.

FOR 6 PEOPLE

1 red cabbage, weighing about 1 kg (2 lb)
1 tablespoon sunflower or groundnut oil
2 - 3 tablespoons red wine vinegar
2 - 3 medium-size eating apples
salt and pepper

Cut the tough outside leaves off the cabbage. Cut it in four and cut out the hard white stalk. Now slice the cabbage finely.

Heat the oil in a large heavy-based pan and toss the cabbage in it for about 5 minutes. Stir in the vinegar.

Peel, core and slice the apples. Add to the cabbage, mixing them together. Add salt and pepper, and water almost to the top of the cabbage. Bring to simmering point, cover and cook, either on top or in a medium-slow oven for two hours.

VARIATIONS ON CLASSIC DISHES

❖ *A variation can be made using fresh or vacuum-packed chestnuts instead of apples: 20 - 25 (peeled, if fresh) should be added to the cabbage.*

❖ *Both versions are nice with roast pork or pork chops.*

PATE LEVEE BRIOCHEE

YEAST PASTRY

This recipe is the one given in a small French publication, 'Petit Recueil de la Gastronomie Alsacienne'. It can be used as a savoury or sweet tart base.

FOR 4 - 6 PEOPLE

10 g (¼ oz) dried yeast (not 'easy-blend')
100 ml (3 ½ fl oz) warm milk
250 g (8 oz) plain flour
1 pinch of salt
40 g (1 ¼ oz) sugar
60 g (2 oz) butter, softened
2 egg whites

Mix the yeast with a little of the warm milk. Put 60 g (2 oz) of the flour in a bowl and make a well into which you put the yeast. Mix together to make a soft starter dough. Cover it with a clean cloth and leave it somewhere warm, not hot, until it doubles in volume (depending on the ambient temperature and humidity, this could take about an hour).

Put the rest of the flour in a bowl. In the middle of it put the salt, sugar, warm milk and the softened butter. Mix all these ingredients, add the egg whites, then the starter dough. Knead by hand until you can see air bubbles and the dough comes away from the side of the bowl. Leave, covered, in a warm place, until it doubles in size, probably between 1 and 2 hours.

When the dough has risen, knead it again for a few minutes, adding a little flour if it is sticky. If you are using it as the base for the plum tart, spread it over an oiled tart tin or baking sheet, arrange the fruit on top, then proceed as described on page 154.

CHOUCROUTE GARNI

PICKLED CABBAGE WITH SMOKED PORK AND SAUSAGES

In the old days, families made their own choucroute, but now it is usually bought ready-prepared from a charcuterie, which also sells the sausages and pork joints to go with it.

The first step is to track down a source of good choucroute (of course you can get it in tins), as well as smoked boiling sausages, such as Strasbourg or the similar Frankfurter sausages, and the salted and smoked pork joints needed. A jambonneau (hock and hand), a neat little ham, is often used, and sometimes carré salé (salted fore loin·in a piece). If no salted pork is available you might consider using some fried pork chops, or roasting a piece of loin of pork or adding some different sausages.

FOR 6 PEOPLE
1.5 kg (3 lb) choucroute
2 medium onions
125 g (4 oz) goose fat or butter
1 large glass of Riesling
250 ml (8 fl oz) stock (chicken stock would be suitable - if no stock is available use water and increase the amount of wine)
1 bay leaf
1 clove garlic
10 juniper berries
6 coriander seeds
salt and pepper

FOR THE GARNISH:
750 g (1½ lb) salted loin of pork

500 - 625 g (1 - 1¼ lb) smoked bacon in a piece
6 medium potatoes, peeled
a jambonneau (see above), if available
6 Strasbourg or Frankfurter sausages
1 small glass of kirsch or other eau de vie, optional

'Wash the *choucroute* in cold water once or twice depending on the season,' it says rather quaintly in a traditional recipe. This is because a large quantity of *choucroute* would be made to last the whole winter - by the end of winter it was likely to be fermenting in the barrel and needed washing very thoroughly.

Drain the *choucroute*, pressing it to squeeze out the moisture. Peel and chop the onions finely, then fry them in the goose fat or butter in a flameproof casserole large enough to hold all the meat. Before the onions brown, add the *choucroute*, tossing it in the fat with a wooden fork for about 15 minutes. Add the glass of wine and some of the stock or water - just enough to moisten it all without the *choucroute* floating in it. Add the bay leaf, garlic, juniper, coriander seeds, salt and pepper. Cover and simmer for about an hour. Stir the *choucroute* and check that it has enough stock, then add the salted pork, if you have it, and the smoked bacon joint to the casserole and cook for another hour. Now put the peeled whole potatoes to cook on top of the *choucroute* for a further half hour. Boil a pan of water to simmer the *jambonneau*, if you have it, and the Strasbourg or Frankfurter sausages for 20 minutes.

Some people add a small glass of kirsch, or one of the other *eaux de vie* liked so much in Alsace, to the *choucroute* just before serving . Pile the *choucroute* up on a dish, arrange slices of the pork joints and the sausages on top and potatoes round the edges. Serve with mustard.

PUREE ROSE

PINK PUREE

This purée is excellent with roasts. You need equal quantities of peeled potatoes and carrots plus butter, milk and seasoning.

Cook the vegetables in salted water, drain and purée. Season and beat in butter and a little warmed milk until you reach the desired smooth, creamy texture. It is a very pretty colour.

Other root vegetables can be added. Turnips and/or celeriac are particularly good. The purée can be made in advance and warmed in a bowl over a pan of simmering water when needed.

SPAETZLE

ALSACE NOODLES

Mimi (or rather, Marie-Léonce) Ling-Freudenreich came third in the Club Prosper Montagne Competition for Coq au Riesling et Spaetzle. Her Spaetzle were voted the best by the jury. This is her recipe. It is enough to accompany one chicken cooked in Riesling.

FOR 6 PEOPLE
*8 eggs
salt
grated nutmeg
500 g (1 lb) flour
2 tablespoons fine semolina
100 ml (3½ fl oz) water
1 tablespoon sunflower or groundnut oil
30 g (1 oz) butter*

Break the eggs in a big bowl. Beat them as though for an omelette. Add salt and a little nutmeg.

Stir in the flour and the semolina little by little, working into the eggs carefully. When they are incorporated, add the glass of water and stir it in. Aim for a consistency between a batter and a dough. Leave to rest for at least an hour.

Get ready a large pan of water. Add salt and a spoonful of oil and bring to the boil. Pour, or press, the flour mixture through a colander or sieve with large holes into the hot water. (As it goes through the holes into the hot water, it turns into worm-like pasta.)

The noodles are cooked when they rise to the top of the pan. Lift them out with a slotted spoon and plunge them into a large bowl of cold water - the water stops them going dry and they swell a little.

When all the noodles have been cooked and cooled, drain them, then sauté them in butter in a frying-pan.

COQ AU RIESLING

CHICKEN IN RIESLING

This is the version used by the Freudenreichs. They serve it with Spaetzle, the Alsace noodles (see above). Try to buy a free-range chicken. Cut it up into portions, or buy chicken joints such as legs (drumstick and thigh attached).

FOR 4 - 6 PEOPLE
*1 chicken, weighing about 1.5 kg (3 lb), jointed
60 g (2 oz) butter
1 tablespoon oil
4 shallots
1 clove garlic
1 small glass cognac
500 ml (15 fl oz) Riesling
sprig parsley and bay leaf
salt, pepper and grated nutmeg
400 ml (14 fl oz) crème fraîche*

Brown the chicken pieces in a mixture of butter and oil in a flameproof casserole. Peel the shallots and garlic and chop finely. Add them to the butter mixture and let them take colour. Warm the cognac in a small pan. Pour it over the chicken and, standing back, ignite carefully. When the flames die down, add the Riesling and the herbs. Bring to simmering point, cover and leave to cook gently for 30 to 45 minutes, until the chicken pieces are tender.

When they are cooked, lift them out and keep them warm. Taste the broth. You could now choose to reduce it by fast boiling for 5 to 10 minutes in order to give it a depth of flavour. If you take this step, add the seasoning afterwards, having tasted again.

Stir in some of the *crème fraîche* and perhaps a little butter. Taste and add more cream until you feel it is right. Sieve the sauce, pour over the chicken and serve.

VARIATIONS ON CLASSIC DISHES
❖ *In some recipes the broth is thickened with flour at the end, and others add an egg yolk as though for a blanquette.*

Baeckaoffa or potée boulangère - an Alsace speciality of mixed meats in Riesling

BAECKAOFFA/POTEE BOULANGERE
CASSEROLE OF MIXED MEATS AND POTATOES

Tradition has it that this dish was made on washing day. Housewives took their casseroles to the baker's oven to cook during the day while they got on with the weekly wash. Hence its name.

There is an oval, glazed, earthenware casserole with lid which is made specially for this in Alsace, but any casserole which has the sort of lid that you can seal with a flour and water paste will be suitable.

FOR 8 PEOPLE
500 g (1 lb) stewing beef
500 g (1 lb) shoulder or leg of pork, boned
500 g (1 lb) shoulder of lamb, boned
1 kg (2 lb) potatoes
500 g (1 lb) carrots
butter for greasing
flour and water for the seal

FOR THE MARINADE:
4 shallots
2 onions
2 cloves garlic
1 - 2 carrots
bouquet garni
salt and pepper
approximately 500 ml (15 fl oz) Riesling

Cut up the meat into cubes. Put all the meat into a bowl with the marinade vegetables, peeled and chopped, the *bouquet garni*, salt, pepper and the wine. Marinate overnight.

Preheat the oven to gas mark 6, 400°F, 200°C.

Peel the potatoes and carrots and slice quite thickly. Butter the casserole. Put in alternate layers of potatoes, carrots and the different meats, seasoning as you go, until you reach the top. You can include the chopped onions, etc. from the marinade if you like. The final layer should be potato.

Pour in the wine from the marinade. It should reach about half-way up the casserole - add more if necessary.

Put on the lid. Mix some flour and water to a sticky paste and seal the lid with this. Bake in the preheated oven for approximately three hours, turning the heat down after the first hour to gas mark 3, 325°F, 160°C.

Break the flour seal carefully so that the bits do not fall into the dish. Serve the *baeckaoffa* with a green salad - anything else would be too heavy.

Plump garlic bulbs in plentiful supply

TARTE AUX QUETSCHS

PLUM TART

This open plum tart uses pâte sablée, a crumbly sweet pastry. The plums are large, oval and dark-skinned: the sort that are used for drying and for cooking, known as Quetsch or Quetsche. They are in season in September, when these tarts are much eaten. Quetschs can be sharp-tasting and therefore will need plenty of sugar. Otherwise, use whatever plums are available and adjust the sugar according to their natural sweetness.

FOR 4 - 6 PEOPLE

*For the pastry to line a 20 cm (8 in) tart tin
(usually with a removable-base and fluted-edges):*

**pinch of salt
3 teaspoons white caster sugar
175 g (6 oz) plain flour, sieved
90 g (3 oz) butter at room temperature
4 tablespoons iced water**

FOR THE FILLING:

**1 kg (2 lb) ripe plums
30 - 60 g (1 - 2 oz) caster sugar
a little powdered cinnamon
icing sugar**

Preheat the oven to gas mark 6, 400°F, 200°C. Put a heavy baking sheet in the middle.

Grease a 20 cm (8 in) tart tin with butter. Add the salt and sugar to the flour in a mixing bowl. Rub the butter into the flour. Add about half the water to moisten - adding more if it seems necessary - the pastry should be crumbly, not sticky and wet. Straightaway make it into a ball and put it into the middle of the buttered tart tin. Use your hands to press it down, spreading it over the base of the tin and gradually up round the edges. Trim off any extra round the edges.

Halve or quarter the plums (depending on size) and take out the stones. Arrange them on the pastry, in concentric circles. The fruit shrinks as it cooks, so it needs to be closely packed. Sprinkle with the sugar and cinnamon. Bake on top of the baking sheet in the preheated oven for 30 to 40 minutes.

When the tart is cooked, slide it out of the tin and onto a cooling rack. It can be served warm or cold with a little icing sugar sprinkled over it.

VARIATIONS ON CLASSIC DISHES

❖ *There is an interesting variation - the tart is made using a pâte levée briochée (see page 149), in other words a yeast-raised pastry with a more cake-like texture, and accompanies a thick homemade vegetable soup. This is not so strange as it might at first seem when it is remembered how many savoury dishes contain prunes. David Ling, the English Export Director of the wine-merchants, Hugel et Fils, in Riquewihr is a convert to this gastronomic curiosity. 'It sounds revolting, but I can assure you, from at-first-reluctant personal experience, it is delicious, and the combination of flavours is phenomenal!'*

Tarte aux quetschs, plum tart

BIBLIOGRAPHY

Adventures on the Wine Route, by Kermit Lynch, published Farrar, Straus & Giroux

Charcuterie and French Pork Cookery, by Jane Grigson, published Penguin

Cooking with de Pomiane, by Edouard de Pomiane, published Faber & Faber

Cooking with Wine, by Robin McDouall, published Penguin

Ethnocuisine de la Bourgogne, by A. Sloimovich, published Cormarin

French Country Cooking, by Elizabeth David, published Penguin

French Provincial Cooking, by Elizabeth David, published Penguin

La Cuisine de France, by Mapie, the Countess de Toulouse-Lautrec, published Orion

La Cuisinière Provençale, by J.-B. Reboul, published Tacussel

Larousse Gastronomique, published Hamlyn

Lulu's Provençal Table, by Richard Olney, published HarperCollins.

Mastering the Art of French Cooking, Vols 1 & 2, by Simone Beck, Louisette Bertholle, Julia Child, published Penguin

Mediterranean Seafood, by Alan Davidson, published Penguin

Modern French Culinary Art, by Henri Paul Pellaprat, published World

On Food and Cooking, the Science and Lore of the Kitchen, by Harold McGee, published George Allen and Unwin Ltd

Petit Recueil de la Gastronomie Alsacienne, by Marguerite Doerflinger, published Editions SAEP

Recettes en Provence, by André Maureau, published Edisud.

Simple French Food, by Richard Olney, published Jill Norman & Hobhouse Ltd

The Escoffier Cook Book, published Crown

RECIPE INDEX